# beading
# BASICS

Carole Rodgers

©2006 Carole Rodgers
Published by

**kp** **krause publications**
*An Imprint of F+W Publications*

**700 East State Street • Iola, WI  54990-0001**
**715-445-2214 • 888-457-2873**

Our toll-free number to place an order or obtain a
free catalog is (800) 258-0929.

Library of Congress Catalog Number: 2005935066

ISBN: 0-89689-170-4

Edited by Maria L. Turner
Designed by Emily Adler
Page layout by Marilyn McGrane

Printed in China

# DEDICATION

In loving memory of my mother, Iris (Lyn) Gardiner, who was the first to teach me to appreciate and enjoy the creative process.

# ACKNOWLEDGMENTS

I am truly grateful to the generous and innovative ladies who let me use photographs of their work in these pages. Their biographies, including which pieces they submitted, are located in the back of the book, page 128.

I also appreciate those who shared their knowledge of beading with me and through me with all of you, the readers. Thank you all so much.

I wish to thank the following companies for their help as well:

- Beacon Adhesives
- Beadalon
- Jay's Indian Arts
- Morning Light Emporium
- One-of-a-Kind Rock Shop
- Wild Things Beads

Lastly, I wish to thank the people at KP Books for making this book happen: editors Maria Turner and Sarah Herman, page designer Emily Adler, cover designer Marilyn McGrane, photographers Bob Best and Kris Kandler, and acquisitions editor Julie Stephani.

# CONTENTS

Introduction ............................................... 6

## Chapter 1: Getting Started ............................ 7

Beads ........................................................................ 8
Supplies and Tools ...................................................... 12

## Chapter 2: Tips and Techniques ..................... 16

Threading Needles ..................................................... 17
Changing Threads and Tying Knots ............................. 17
Breaking a Bead ........................................................ 19
Using a Stop Bead ...................................................... 19
Using Split Rings ........................................................ 19
Ending a Strand ......................................................... 20
Using Head Pins ........................................................ 21
Using Eye Pins ........................................................... 22
Using Wrapped Pins ................................................... 23
Working with Memory Wire ........................................ 24
Working with Wire ..................................................... 24
Weaving on a Loom ................................................... 25
Creating Woven Chains ............................................... 27
   • Daisy Chain ...................................................... 27
   • Ladder Stitch ..................................................... 29
   • Spiral Rope ....................................................... 31
   • Lacy Spiral ........................................................ 32
   • Potawatomi Stitch ............................................. 33
Using Weaving Stitches ............................................... 34
   • Right-Angle Weave ........................................... 34
   • Peyote Stitch (Gourd Stitch) ............................... 36
   • Vertical Netting (Lattice Weave) .......................... 37
   • Square Stitch .................................................... 39

## Chapter 3: Design Principles and Color Theory .............. 40

Symmetrical Patterns ................................... 41
Asymmetrical Patterns ................................. 41
Random Patterns ........................................ 42
Repeating ................................................. 42
Color Theory ............................................. 43

# Chapter 4: Projects ....................................... 45

Purple and Pearls Jewelry Set (Simple One-Strand Stringing).................. 46

Elegant Eyeglasses Holders (Simple One-Strand Stringing) ..................... 49

Fun and Funky Elastic Bracelets (Simple One-Strand Stringing)..............52

   • Fruit Bead Bracelet...............................................53

   • Mexican Cups Bracelet .......................................... 54

   • Boulder Opal Beads Bracelet ............................... 55

Multi-Strand Bracelets (Multi-Strand Stringing) ..............................56

   • Pretty Pearls Bracelet.......................................... 57

   • Toffee and Topaz Bracelet.................................. 58

   • Copper Flashes Bracelet .................................... 60

Illusion Necklace (Multi-Strand Stringing)................................. 62

Coral and Turquoise Necklace (Using Multiple-Hole Beads)................. 64

Decorative Spacers Bracelets (Using Multiple-Hole Beads)................. 67

Cinnabar Set (Using Head/Eye Pins) ...................................... 70

Teal and Crystal Earrings (Using Head/Eye Pins) .......................... 72

Ball Chain Necklace and Earrings (Using Head/Eye Pins) ................. 74

Wine Glass Tags (Using Memory Wire) .................................... 76

Two-Strand Memory Wire Bracelets (Using Memory Wire) ................ 78

   • Red-and-Silver Bracelet..................................... 79

   • Black Facets Bracelet ...................................... 80

   • Turquoise Bracelet........................................... 81

Star Ornaments (Beads and Wirework) ................................... 82

Bead-Embellished Shirt (Bead Embroidery) ............................... 85

Beaded Lampshade (Bead Embroidery).................................... 88

Mookite Necklace (Simple Beaded Cabochon) ............................ 92

Loomed Brooch (Loom Weaving) ......................................... 95

Loomed Bracelets (Loom Weaving)........................................ 98

   • Lavender Loomed Bracelet................................... 99

   • Pink-and-Blue Loomed Bracelet........................... 100

   • Designer Mix Loomed Bracelet ........................... 101

Art Glass Daisy Chain Necklace (Woven Chains) ......................... 102

Ladder Stitch Cat Collar Necklace (Woven Chains) ...................... 105

Spiral Rope Jewelry Set (Woven Chains) ................................ 108

Dutch Spiral Shell Necklace (Woven Chains) ............................ 110

Embellished Potawatomi Bracelet (Woven Chains) ....................... 112

Right-Angle Weave Yellow Jade Jewelry Set (Weaving Stitches) .......... 115

Peyote Bracelet (Weaving Stitches) ...................................... 118

Square Stitch Candleholders (Weaving Stitches) ......................... 120

Netting Wine Bottle Cover (Weaving Stitches) ........................... 122

Gallery .....125    Resources and Contributors..... 128

# INTRODUCTION

Looking back on my first trip to a bead store more than a decade ago, I remember being amazed at the endless possibilities that lay before me. There was such a confusion of light and color that I barely knew where to look first. I wanted everything I saw.

After much deliberation, I bought a few tubes of beads and proudly left with my prizes. I had no earthly idea what I was going to do with them so I put them away.

It wasn't long before I was searching out the information I needed to be able to make jewelry with my beads. I bought books, took classes and picked the brains of people whose work I liked.

Over the years, I've managed to figure out how to do most everything I wanted to do in beading through one of these methods. It sure would have been nice to have all the information in one place, though.

With that in mind, I have geared this volume to the beginner. I have tried to write and illustrate it in such a way that it can be used as a quick reference. The projects are lessons in how to use the material, finding or technique discussed.

Because it is impossible for every bead store to carry every bead, you probably will not be able to purchase the same beads I've used. I've tried to do the projects in a way that you can substitute beads of similar shapes or sizes. Several variations are given for each technique because using different beads can result in an entirely different look.

I hope you find this book a useful guide as you start on your beading adventure.

*Carole Rodgers*

# GETTING STARTED

This chapter covers the terminology and the basic materials you will need to begin beading. You will not use all of these items on every project, but if you do a lot of beading, you will eventually use most of them. Buy what you need as you need it, and add to your tools and materials as you can. When it comes to findings and stringing materials, it is always wise to purchase extra. Mistakes are not uncommon when you are learning, and some things cannot be reused.

# BEADS

The most basic material needed when making beaded jewelry is, of course, beads. The variety of beads available is so large that it's impossible to describe all of them. The following are the most common materials and processes presently used in beadmaking. From bone to precious stone, each has its own personality.

## BEAD MATERIALS

**Bone:** A popular bead material that can be carved, ground, painted or dyed. Bone beads are usually lightweight.

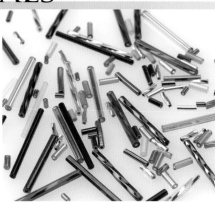

**Bugle beads:** Long, thin glass tube beads from 2mm to 30mm long in a variety of finishes. They can be straight, twisted or hex-cut.

**Faceted:** Any bead that is ground with one or more flat surfaces. Faceting is most commonly done on glass, precious or semiprecious stone beads.

**Gemstone and semiprecious:** Semi-precious gemstones are carved or ground into beads. They come in a large variety of colors, sizes and shapes.

**Lampworked or artisan:** Lampworked beads are handmade by artisans one at a time through a process of wrapping molten glass around a mandrel in an open flame.

**Metal:** Beads can be made from a variety of different metals. Many used in jewelry are made from precious metals or are a base metal plated with precious metals. Like glass beads, they can be molded into a large variety of shapes.

KEEP IN MIND THAT MOST BEADS ARE IMPORTED AND MANY COME FROM SMALL FACTORIES. IT IS WISE TO BUY MORE BEADS THAN YOU THINK YOU WILL NEED TO FINISH ANY PROJECT. DIFFERENCES CAN OCCUR IN GLASS DYE LOTS, SO EVEN THOUGH TWO BEADS MAY HAVE THE SAME NUMBER OR COLOR DESCRIPTION, THEY CAN BE TWO DIFFERENT COLORS. IN ADDITION, SOME BEADS ARE MANUFACTURED FOR ONLY A SHORT TIME AND ONCE THEY ARE SOLD OUT, YOU MAY NEVER FIND THEM AGAIN. FINALLY, BUYING EXTRA BEADS IS SIMPLY ECONOMICAL AND WILL PREVENT THE AGGRAVATION OF HAVING TO MAKE ANOTHER TRIP TO THE BEAD STORE TO GET A FEW BEADS TO FINISH YOUR PROJECT.

**tip**

**Plastic:** A material readily used in bead production, although not popular for high-end jewelry. It can imitate any number of materials, like gemstones and glass.

**Polymer clay:** Beads from polymer clay are becoming more widely available in bead shops. They are often artisan-made. Many are made from canes like millefiori glass and have interesting patterns. Such clay can duplicate other materials, like bone and semiprecious stone.

**Pressed glass:** Beads molded when the glass is still soft. They can be made in almost any size or shape. Many beads used in costume jewelry are pressed glass.

**Shell:** Shell can be ground into shapes, dyed and treated in a number of ways to make interesting beads. Small whole shells are often used for beads by drilling a hole in them.

**Swarovski crystals:** These crystal beads are made in Austria. The beads have a high lead content and are precision faceted. They have a sparkle that resembles diamonds.

**Wood:** These beads are made from any number of different wood types and are often carved, painted or dyed. Like bone, wooden beads are relatively lightweight.

# SEED BEADS

Seed beads are very small, like seeds — hence their name. The two kinds of seed beads I recommend for bead weaving are Czech and Japanese. These two are more uniform in size than those from other countries. With a few exceptions, the seed beads used in this book are all Japanese. In complicated bead weaving, it's often necessary to pass through the bead multiple times. Japanese seed beads have larger holes to facilitate the extra thread.

There are a number of sizes of seed beads used in this book — 6°, 8° and 11°. Seed beads are sized by a number with an "°" symbol behind it, or sometimes with a "/0" behind the number. This symbol stands for "ought" and comes from an old way of numbering beads. Just remember that the larger the number, the smaller the bead.

## Bead Finishes

Seed beads are available in a wide range of finishes, and more are being developed all the time. These different finishes are used on glass beads, as well. The following list is a brief reference to the most common bead finishes.

**Aurora borealis (AB) or iridescent:** These beads have a permanent rainbow-colored finish.

**Galvanized metallic:** The metallic coating on these beads is very thin and will wear off in time. Do not use these beads in anything that will be handled or worn.

**Lined:** Instead of a silver lining, these beads have a color (usually different from the glass color) painted inside the holes.

**Luster/lustre:** Beads with a transparent, colored coating. The finish is often called Ceylon. Pearl beads have this finish.

**Matte:** The dull finish on these beads is made by etching or tumbling.

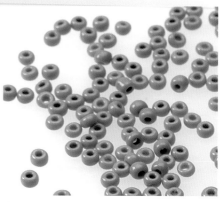

**Opaque:** Solid-colored beads, often seen in Native American beadwork.

**Plated metallic:** Beads with a metal plating. They retain their color well and are expensive.

**Silver-lined:** Transparent beads with a silver lining in the holes. They are very bright and shiny, though the silver may tarnish or wear off over time.

**Surface-dyed:** Process used on all sorts of beads to make difficult colors like purple and pink. The color can wear off or fade with time and use. Do not use these beads on any project that will be worn or handled a lot.

**Transparent:** Clear or colored see-through glass.

**White hearts:** Colored glass around a white center (heart).

# SUPPLIES AND TOOLS

The following supplies and tools are used when you are ready to make that gorgeous creation. As with beads, when it comes to buying findings, threads and needles, try to have more available than you think you will need.

## FINDINGS

"Findings" is the term generally used for all the hardware needed to finish a piece of jewelry. Findings come in both base and precious metals. You will need some of the following basic findings before you start. You may want to begin with the less expensive base metal parts until you get proficient at using them.

**Bead tip:** Used at the ends of bead strands mostly to hide the knot. (I prefer bottom-hole clamshell tips that close around the knot to hide it from view.)

**Clasp:** A closure used to join the ends of the piece of jewelry together. The most commonly used clasps are toggles that consist of a bar and a loop, spring rings and lobster claws.

CLASPS.

**Crimp bead:** Small, soft metal bead in a silver or gold color and of varying size that is crimped around the bead wire to hold the strand to a clasp or other part of the jewelry.

**Earring finding:** Available in a variety of configurations like wires, ball and post, and clips. Hoops are available to attach to the findings as well.

**Eye pin:** Pin that has an eye already turned on one end and often used to link two things together.

JUMP RINGS.

**Head pin:** Long, straight pin with a flat head on one end, like a straight pin without a point.

**Jump ring:** Small ring of wire, sized in millimeters, used to join parts of a piece of jewelry together.

**Pendant bail:** Decorative loop used to attach a pendant to a chain or beaded strand.

**Pin back:** Attached to the back of a piece to make a brooch. They are available in different lengths.

SPLIT RINGS.

**Split ring:** Double jump ring that looks like a very tight spring and will not split apart if it has tension on it.

BEAD TIPS.

**Strand spacer:** Bar with a number of holes used to hold the strands apart.

PIN BACKS.

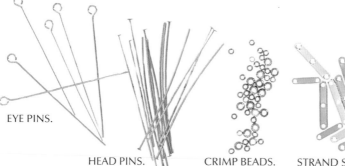

EYE PINS.

HEAD PINS.

CRIMP BEADS.

STRAND SPACERS.

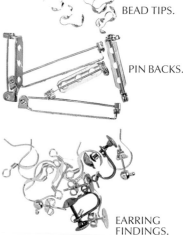

EARRING FINDINGS.

# NEEDLES

When beading, you can use any needle that will go through the bead. A heavier needle is nice when stringing larger beads with larger holes. Use beading needles when bead weaving or when using smaller beads.

**Beading:** These needles are thinner and longer than regular sewing needles, ranging from size 10 to size 22, with 22 being the thinnest. The size numbers loosely refer to the size of beads that they will pass through. They also come in different lengths. Because beading needles are so thin, they bend easily. Keep a number on hand. A size 10 or 12 needle will work for most beading in this book.

**Sharps:** Short, sharp pointed needles used for bead embroidery that are also useful for cabochon beading on leather. A size 10 or 12 needle is a good choice.

**Tapestry:** Blunt pointed needles used for counted embroidery and are also useful for stringing larger beads. A size 26 is a good choice.

**Wire beading:** Fine, twisted wire needles with a loop where the eye should be. This needle is used for thicker threads, like silk knotting cord. The loop collapses on the first pass through a bead.

# GLUES

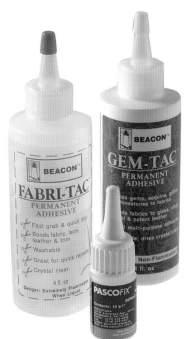

The three main glues used for these projects are shown here and are my favorites. They are, however, just three glues of many that are available.

**Fabri-Tac™:** Used to attach leather to leather.

**Gem-Tac™:** Used to attach stones and metal pieces to leather and other surfaces.

**Pasco® Fix Industrial Adhesive:** Used to adhere metal balls on the end of memory wire and to adhere metal parts together.

# THREADS AND STRINGING MATERIALS

Different threads have different strengths, which is an important factor in choosing the type of thread to use for beading. Use the strongest thread possible for the effect you want to achieve. The thread used in each project in this book will be given in the materials list.

**Braided filament:** Made of multiple filaments braided together into an exceptionally strong thread, it is available in several diameters, has almost no stretch, resists abrasion and is difficult to cut with regular scissors (use blade scissors instead). It is also 100 percent water resistant and will not rot in water like other threads. It is not available in a lot of colors, generally just white, gray and green, but it can be colored with permanent marking pens.

**Kevlar:** Incredibly strong thread used in making bulletproof vests. It is naturally yellow and can be dyed darker with regular fabric dyes.

**Memory wire:** Rigid, pre-coiled steel wire that remembers its coiled shape. It is available in necklace, bracelet and ring sizes.

**Nymo:** Probably the most common thread used for beading. It is made of non-twisted bonded nylon filaments, resists mildew, and doesn't rot. It comes in a variety of thickness and colors and is available in sizes designated by letters OO, O, B, and D, with OO being the thinnest and D the thickest. It stretches a little, so it is wise to give the piece of thread a gentle pull to remove part of the stretch before starting to bead.

**Silamide:** Twisted nylon tailoring thread with a waxy feel that is widely used for bead weaving. It is available in a variety of colors and is similar to Nymo O in thickness.

**Stringing wire:** Usually made of a number of strands of extremely fine wire twisted together and then coated with a plastic film to prevent tarnishing. These wires work well for stringing larger beads and beads with sharp edges that might cut nylon or silk threads. One benefit of string wire is that it doesn't require a needle.

**Thread conditioner:** Beeswax product used on thread to keep it from tangling.

# Tools

There are a number of tools that all beaders should have. Buy the best quality tools you can afford and learn to use them correctly. Good tools are usually easier to use, break less often, and provide better quality results.

**Bead gauge:** A sliding ruler that accurately measures the size of beads in inches and millimeters. It is not essential, but can be quite helpful.

**Bead sorting dish:** A ceramic, plastic or metal dish, or set of triangle dishes, to pour beads into to keep them separated as you work. Some beaders lay beads on a piece of felt, suede, Ultrasuede® or Velux™. The rough surface of these materials keeps the beads from moving around and makes them easier to catch with the needle.

**Chain nose pliers:** Pliers with wider, smooth jaws that do not taper down to sharp points and are used for bending wire at right-angles.

**Crimp pliers:** Pliers designed specifically for doing a professional job of attaching crimp beads. It works in a two-step process whereby the bead is first crimped around the wire and then folded over back onto itself. See Chapter 2 on page 20 for more information on using crimp beads and pliers.

**Needle nose pliers:** Pliers that look like a semicircle from the end and have jaws that are long and taper to a blunt point.

**Round nose pliers:** Pliers with smooth, round jaws that taper to fine points. Used for making wire loops, like in the ends of head and eye pins.

**Scissors:** Used for cutting thread.

**Split ring pliers:** Pliers designed to be used with split rings; they separate the rings to make it easier to attach other items.

**Tool or storage box:** A place to keep works in progress and other tools and materials. Although a personal decision, the fishing tackle section of many stores provides a wide variety of portable storage solutions.

**Wire cutter:** Tool that looks like a pair of pliers but is specifically used for cutting wire, such as stringing wire.

# TIPS AND TECHNIQUES

My beading education mostly came from books. When I started beading, few classes were being given where I lived at the time. A number of things were not covered in books, like finishing ends nicely, good knots to use, changing threads and even how to set up a workspace. This chapter includes numerous tips I've learned over the years to help make your jewelry look professional.

# THREADING NEEDLES

If you have a problem threading the needle, dampen the end of thread and smooth it between your thumb and index fingernails. It will spread out slightly and get a little thinner, which will help it pass through the eye more easily. The closer you hold the thread to its end, the easier it is to insert it into the needle.

Where there are references to "single-thread the needle," just use one strand of thread. "Double-threading" means to pull the thread through the needle until the thread ends meet and the needle is centered.

# CHANGING THREADS AND TYING KNOTS

In bead weaving, sooner or later you will run out of thread in the middle of your work. My favorite way to add a new thread is to use a weaver's knot. If you get proficient at using this knot, you can change threads in the middle of a project without it being noticeable. Here's how:

## Weaver's Knot

A weaver's knot is a very effective way to join two threads together in the middle of a project.

**1.** Cross A (the end of the old thread) and B (the end of the new thread) and hold between thumb and forefinger at point C (Figure 2-1). D is the new thread.

**2.** Pass D around and over A, up under B and over A again (Figure 2-2).

**3.** Turn A down over D, over the new thread B and through the loop made by D (Figure 2-3).

**4.** Bring end B down and hold it with end A. Pull D tight, making sure you have pulled A down to where you want the knot. This knot slips through most seed beads and holds very well without being glued.

**5.** Weave the old end back through the work once you have tied on the new thread, being sure to tie an overhand knot after a few beads.

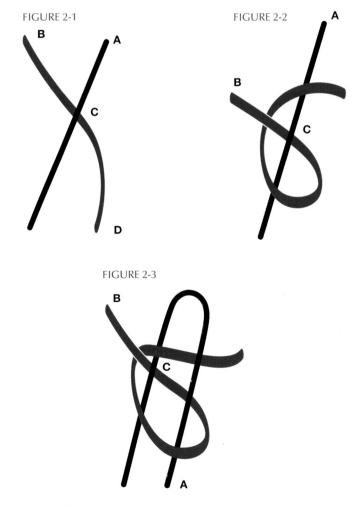

FIGURE 2-1

FIGURE 2-2

FIGURE 2-3

## FIGURE 2-4

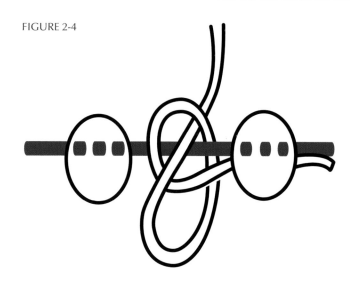

# Overhand Knot

Overhand knots are used most to weave in thread ends.

**1.** Take a small stitch over a thread between two beads in your work and pull the thread through until you have just a small loop of thread left.

**2.** Pass the needle through the loop (Figure 2-4) and pull the thread tight.

**3.** Pass through a few beads and tie another overhand knot.

**4.** Apply a very small amount of glue to the thread close to the knot and pass through a few more beads.

**5.** Pull the thread tight and cut off the excess thread close to a bead.

## FIGURE 2-5

## FIGURE 2-6

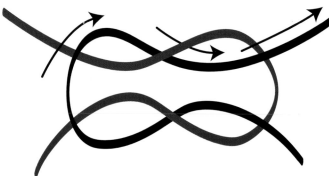

# Square Knot

A square knot is a good knot for ending threads and can also be used to change threads in the middle of a piece.

**1.** Cross the thread in your right hand over the thread in your left hand, bring around and then through to tie the knot (Figure 2-5).

**2.** Take the thread that's now in your left hand over the thread in your right hand, bring around and then through to tie another knot (Figure 2-6).

**3.** Put a small amount of glue on the knot to make sure it stays secure.

## FIGURE 2-7

# Surgeon's Knot

This knot is a lot like a square knot, only stronger, because it has an extra loop-through.

**1.** Cross the right end of the thread over the left and pass through the loop.

**2.** Pass through again and pull the ends to tighten.

**3.** Cross the left thread end over the right, pass through once and tighten (Figure 2-7).

# BREAKING A BEAD

Occasionally, you will get a bead in the wrong spot. If it is a seed bead, it's usually easier to break the bead than tear out your work. You want to be very careful when breaking a bead, though. If you use pliers and attempt to smash it, you will break the thread. To avoid thread breaks, try the following method:

1. Tighten the thread over your finger so the bead pops up away from the thread.

2. Grab the bead with the middle of your pliers, perpendicular to the hole and above the thread.

3. Turn your face away and squeeze the pliers until the bead breaks.

SAFETY TIP: I USUALLY BREAK BEADS OVER A WASTEBASKET OR UNDER A TOWEL TO AVOID FLYING GLASS. IF YOU MUST LOOK, BE SURE TO WEAR PROTECTIVE EYE GEAR. GLASS IN THE EYE IS NOT FUN!

**tip**

# USING A STOP BEAD

A stop bead is tied on close to the end of the thread to keep beads from slipping off the thread. Simply tie it on with a half-knot so that it can easily be undone later. You will later remove the bead and use the thread to finish the project.

# USING SPLIT RINGS

Split rings are used when a secure link, usually between the bead strand(s) and the clasp, is desired. The rings themselves, however, can be a challenge to work with—unless you use a split ring pliers. Here's how:

1. Use the bent nose of the pliers to separate the rings close to the end of the ring (Figure 2-8).

2. Slip the loop of the clasp between the wires while holding the ring apart.

3. Use jewelry pliers to move the clasp around the length of the ring until the clasp is loose in the split ring (Figure 2-9).

FIGURE 2-8

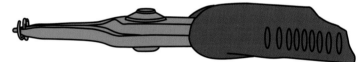

FIGURE 2-9

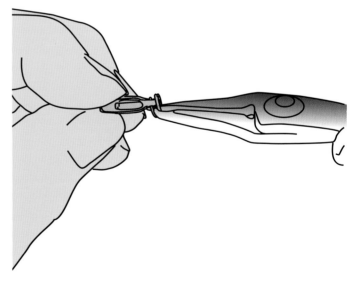

# ENDING A STRAND

I have tried a number of ways to end my beaded strands so they look professional. I find that the following methods work best for me.

## Option 1

1. If you use bead wire for the strand, end that strand by threading on a crimp bead, passing through the clasp or jump/split ring and passing back through the crimp bead into the bead strand. Be sure to pull the wire snug.

2. Using the crimp pliers in the "W" hole, bend the crimp bead tightly around the wire to secure (Figure 2-10).

3. Put the crimped bead in the "O" hole of the pliers, press down and fold the bead over onto itself to secure (Figure 2-11).

4. Work wire through the beading for about ½" and trim the end so it is hidden in the bead strand.

## Option 2

1. Make the closure an integral part of the beaded piece by beading a loop at the end of one strand.

2. Attach a button or large bead on the other end to hook the loop over.

## Option 3

For longer necklaces—ones that will slip easily over the head—I often skip the clasp entirely. The clasp-less strand is actually more comfortable to wear, especially on a bare neck.

## Option 4 (My Favorite)

1. Pass thread through crimp bead and tie several square knots around the crimp bead.

2. Take thread through bottom hole of clamshell bead tip (Figures 2-12A and 2-12B) to begin necklace.

3. Glue the knots, trim the threads and close the clamshell around the crimp bead (Figure 2-13).

4. Bend the bar of the clamshell tip around in a loop (Figure 2-14).

## Option 5

1. When using heavier thread or bead wire, thread a crimp bead before threading on the clamshell bead tip.

2. String on a second crimp bead.

3. Pass thread or wire back through the clamshell tip hole, the first crimp bead and back through the beading.

4. Secure the crimp bead on the strand.

5. Trim thread or wire ends.

6. Close the clamshell around the second crimp bead.

FIGURE 2-10

FIGURE 2-11

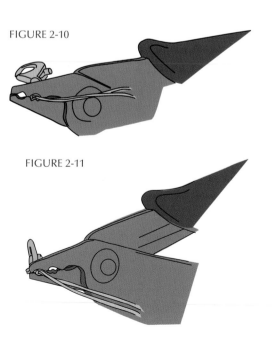

FIGURE 2-12A

FIGURE 2-12B

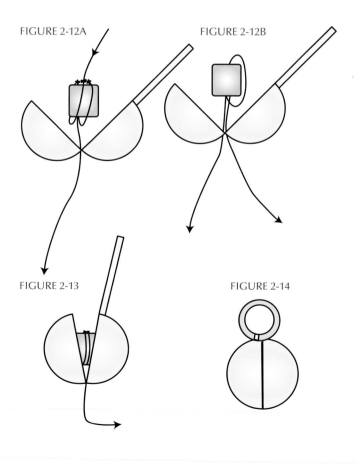

FIGURE 2-13

FIGURE 2-14

# USING HEAD PINS

Head pins look like large, blunt straight pins (Figure 2-15). They are used to thread beads on to make drops for earrings or to suspend off necklaces as in a pendant. Sometimes, they are used at the ends of bracelets to make a decorative dangle.

Head pins can be purchased in plated base metals, silver or gold and in a variety of lengths. Most of the head pins used in this book are the less expensive plated ones. If you wish to use silver or gold, buy the correct length for your project so you won't waste precious metal. The pins also come in hard and soft metals. The harder ones will hold their shape better. Follow the instructions and graphics to see how to use a head pin correctly.

**1.** Thread the beads on the pin, making sure to allow ³⁄₈" of headroom above the beads.

**2.** Use straight pliers to bend the ³⁄₈" excess at a right-angle to the body of the pin (Figure 2-16). It is best to make the bend tight above the beads.

**3.** Grab the very end of the pin between the jaws of a round nose pliers and while holding the pin with other hand, curve the end of the pin around the nose of the pliers in the direction of the bend to form a ring. (Figure 2-17).

**4.** Complete step 3 so the pliers or pin will end up upside-down, as shown (Figure 2-18). Be sure to get the end of the pin around snugly against the straight bar of the pin so there is very little space between them.

**5.** Finish the pin to look like that shown (Figure 2-19). Practice a few times until you feel comfortable with this process.

THESE EARRINGS ARE ALL MADE WITH HEAD PINS.

FIGURE 2-15    FIGURE 2-16    FIGURE 2-17

(Arrow denotes direction of curve.)

FIGURE 2-18    FIGURE 2-19

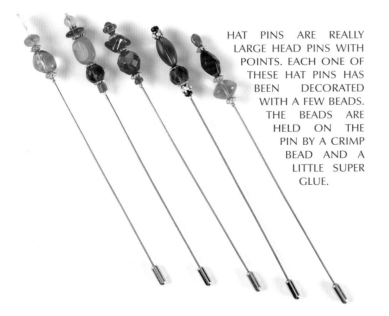

HAT PINS ARE REALLY LARGE HEAD PINS WITH POINTS. EACH ONE OF THESE HAT PINS HAS BEEN DECORATED WITH A FEW BEADS. THE BEADS ARE HELD ON THE PIN BY A CRIMP BEAD AND A LITTLE SUPER GLUE.

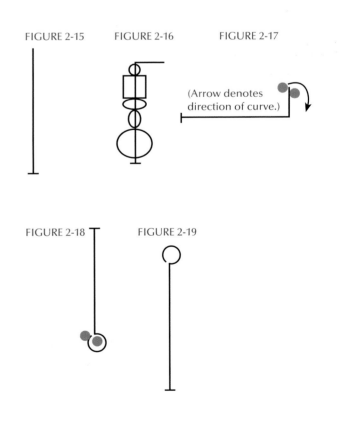

21

# USING EYE PINS

Eye pins look a lot like head pins, but they have a loop on one end instead of the flat head (Figure 2-20). Eye pins are used to join two things together. They come in the same materials and lengths as head pins. Follow the instructions and graphics to see how to use an eye pin correctly.

**1.** Thread on beads, making sure to allow ⅜" headroom above the beads.

**2.** Use straight pliers to bend the end of the eye pin at a right-angle to the pin ⅜" from the end (Figure 2-21). Be sure to bend the pin so it is lined up with the loop. If you don't, the pin will be twisted and won't work correctly in your designs.

**3.** Grab the very end of the pin between the jaws of a round nose pliers and while holding the pin with the other hand, curve the end of the pin around the nose of the pliers toward the bend to make a ring (Figure 2-22).

**4.** Complete step 3 so the pliers or pin will end up upside-down, as shown (Figure 2-23). Be sure to get the end of the pin around snugly against the straight bar of the pin so there is very little space between them.

**5.** Finish the pin to look like that shown (Figure 2-24). Done correctly, the eye pin will lay flat on the table. Practice making a few eye pins before starting your project.

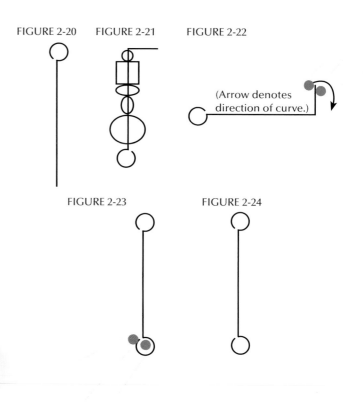

FIGURE 2-20    FIGURE 2-21    FIGURE 2-22

(Arrow denotes direction of curve.)

FIGURE 2-23    FIGURE 2-24

THESE TWO FAN PULLS ARE DONE ON GLORIFIED HEAD/ EYE PINS. EACH COMES WITH A DECORATIVE LOOP ON THE END. ALL YOU HAVE TO DO IS THREAD ON A FEW BEADS, TURN A LOOP ON THE OTHER END AND ATTACH TO THE BALL CHAIN. NOTE THE ONE AT THE TOP HAS A HEAD PIN WITH BEADS FOR A DANGLE.

# USING WRAPPED PINS

A wrapped pin is the most secure way to put beads on a head or eye pin. It is also the most difficult to make. You will need to choose a pin that is at least 1" to 1½" longer than the length you need. Follow the instructions and graphics to see how to make a wrapped pin.

**1.** Thread beads on a head pin, leaving 1" to 1½" headroom above the beads.

**2.** Place a chain nose pliers around the post and sitting on the beads so there is about ³/₁₆" under the pliers.

**3.** Bend remainder of post at a right-angle (Figure 2-25).

**4.** Use a round nose pliers to turn a loop against the bend on the pin (Figure 2-26).

**5.** Hold loop with one pair of pliers and grab the end of the pin with another pair to wrap the excess pin around the post.

**6.** Trim excess wire close to the pin to look like that shown (Figure 2-27). As with head and eye pins, creating wrapped pins will take some practice.

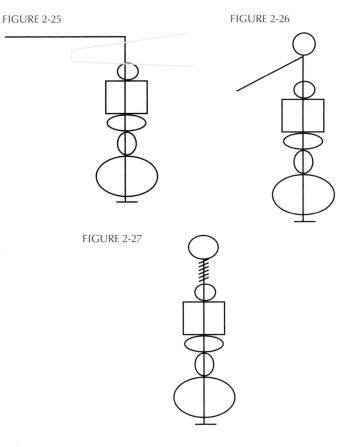

FIGURE 2-25

FIGURE 2-26

FIGURE 2-27

THIS COPPER SPARKLES NECKLACE FEATURES THREE POLYMER CLAY BEADS BY DENISE MILLER. THE CENTER ONE IS SUSPENDED FROM A DECORATIVE WRAPPED PIN MADE OF COPPER WIRE. THE WIRE END IS COILED, BEADS ARE THREADED ON AND THEN A LOOP IS TURNED AND WRAPPED.

# WORKING WITH MEMORY WIRE

Memory wire is a marvelous product to use in making jewelry. Memory wire is a hard, yet springy, coiled steel wire that retains its shape. It resembles a slinky.

Memory wire comes in several sizes: ring wire, two sizes of bracelet wire and necklace wire.

Originally, you had to turn a loop on the end of memory wire to hold the beads in place. Now, however, it's possible to buy special ends that have been half-drilled to glue on the ends of the wire. These ends make for an attractive and professional looking project.

One important thing to remember about memory wire is to never cut it with regular wire cutters. Because the wire is so hard, it will ruin most wire cutters. Instead, hold it with your pliers where you want to cut it. Then bend the memory wire back and forth against the pliers until it snaps. A fine file will remove any burrs that might result at the breaking point.

There are also a variety of memory wire cutters available, but be aware they may not hold up all that well with repeated use.

MEMORY WIRE COMES IN SIZES APPROPRIATE FOR NECKLACES, BRACELETS AND RINGS, AS SHOWN. THERE ARE ALSO SEVERAL OPTIONS FOR END CAPS, WHICH ALSO CAN BE SEEN ABOVE.

# WORKING WITH WIRE

Beads and wire are an excellent combination. You can use wire as you do thread, but wire goes beyond what you can do with thread. Because wire is stiffer, you can do all sorts of structural projects. Freestanding flowers, ornaments and even baskets are possible when using wire.

Working with wire is relatively easy. There are a few things you need to remember, though. Wire has memory. Since it usually comes coiled on a spool, it has a tendency to kink. Cut the piece of wire and run it gently through your fingers several times to smooth it. When you pull it through the beads, do so slowly and watch to make sure it doesn't kink as you pull through. If it starts to kink, back out, put your finger in the loop and pull over your finger or something round like a pencil, and pull through gently.

Wire is sold in gauges. The larger the gauge number the thinner the wire; 18-gauge is much thicker than 32-gauge. For most beading projects, you would use wire in the 24- to 34-gauge range.

WIRE PROVIDES A DURABILITY TO PROJECTS, LIKE THIS SNOWFLAKE ORNAMENT, THAT CANNOT BE OBTAINED WHEN WORKING WITH THREAD AND BEADS.

# WEAVING ON A LOOM

Weaving beads on a loom is an old craft and has been used by Native Americans for many years. It is a quick way to make larger articles in beading, such as purses, wall hangings, belts and jewelry.

There are a couple of down-sides to looming, though. You have to set up (warp) the loom and when you are finished you have to hide the warp threads. If your project is large, this can take a considerable amount of time.

Looms are made in a number of sizes and configurations. If you want to make bracelets like the projects in this book, the inexpensive looms sold at hobby stores will suffice. If you want to do larger projects, you will need to explore the market and find the correct one for you. You may end up needing several looms for different types of projects.

Although the configuration of looms may vary, the way they work is the same. They have a means to secure the long threads, called warp threads. (See the hooks on either end of the sample loom.) They all have a way to keep the warp threads separated by equal distances. This sample loom uses a fine spring. Some looms are adjustable for length. The sample loom also is static, which makes it useful for small projects like the brooch and bracelets projects on pages 95 through 101.

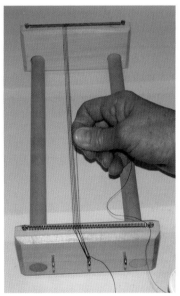

A STANDARD-SIZED TABLE LOOM, LIKE THE ONE SHOWN AT THE LEFT, IS ALL THAT IS NEEDED FOR COMPLETING THE LOOMED PROJECTS IN THIS BOOK.

## Weaving a Bracelet

### Threading the Loom

**1.** Choose beading thread that matches the beads. Note: Here, black thread is used so it shows up better in the photographs.

**2.** Tie the end of the thread on the center hook at one end of the loom, as shown. If you have a larger project, you might need to use all three hooks.

**3.** Pass the thread end through the spring on the end of the loom closest to where the thread was tied and just left of center.

**4.** Take the thread to the other side of the loom and pass through the spring in approximately the same place.

**5.** Pass the thread down and around the center hook on the other end.

**6.** Bring the thread end back up and through the spring in the next slot to the right, keeping tension on the thread for a tight weave. Note: To adjust for bead size, you may need to move over one slot. Two slots are used here for the 8° beads.

**7.** Continue moving up and down the loom in the same manner until there is one more thread than the pattern is wide. You will need eight threads for this project. When bead weaving, you always will need one more thread than you have for the finished bead pattern.

**8.** When all threads are in place, tie the thread end on the hook and clip the thread from the spool.

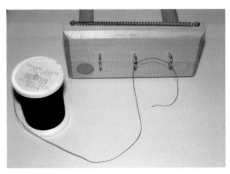

STEP 2

STEP 7

25

## Weaving the Bead Pattern

1. Single-thread a beading needle with 1 yard of thread.

2. Determine where to start the beading pattern to center it on the loom threads. In this case, the throat of this loom is 11" long and the pattern is 6" long. Start beading 2½" from one end of the loom (11 minus 6 = 5 and 5 divided by 2 = 2½).

3. Tie the end of the thread with an overhand knot to one side of the warp near where you intend to start beading, as shown. Tie it on the left side if you are right-handed and right side if you are left-handed. This new thread will become the weft thread.

4. Pour the beads for the pattern into a bead sorting dish.

5. Refer to the pattern and thread the beads corresponding to the first row of the pattern onto the needle. You may start at top or bottom of the pattern. Just be sure to maintain that progression.

6. Pass beads to end of thread and then take them under the warp thread, popping beads up between warp threads so you have a warp thread on either side of every bead, as shown. Press down on warp threads with your thumb while popping beads up with your forefinger.

7. Pass the needle through the beads from right to left (opposite, if left-handed) and pull the weft thread through, as shown. Be careful not to pierce the warp threads with the needle. The beads are now sandwiched between the weft threads and separated by the warp threads.

8. Repeat steps 5 through 7, following the pattern.

9. Continue weaving the pattern until close to the end of the thread and then tie the thread off on the far left (or right) warp thread after passing the needle through the beads, as shown.

10. Start a new thread just as in steps 1 and 3 above. All thread ends will be worked in after removing the piece from the loom.

11. Continue weaving until the desired bracelet length is finished.

## Finishing the Bracelet

1. Clip the threads loose from the hooks of the loom on both ends.

2. Add clasp, as detailed in each individual loom project, pages 99 through 101.

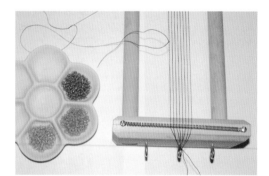

STEP 3

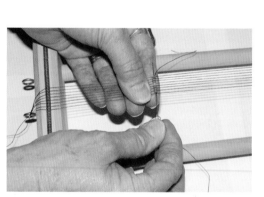

STEP 5

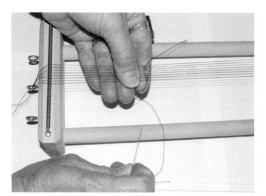

STEP 6

STEP 8

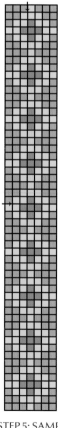

STEP 5: SAMPLE PATTERN

# CREATING WOVEN CHAINS

The term bead weaving encompasses any type of beading in which you pass through some or all of the beads more than once. This includes the loom weaving done in the previous section. The stitches that follow do not need a loom, so they are called off-loom weaving stitches.

First, we'll focus on a number of weaving stitches that make lovely beaded chains. You can use them numerous ways in jewelry and home decor items. Their possible use is unlimited. Although all of these chains are lovely alone, you can use them to showcase a beautiful handmade bead or pendant.

In the projects sections, there are several bracelets done with the basic stitch to show how different beads change the look of the stitch. Due to space constraints, instructions are given for the basic stitch or stitches and one feature project. For best results before trying the featured project, practice the basic stitches detailed here. Make a bracelet length and add a clasp or button-and-loop closing. There's no reason your practice pieces can't become functional and lovely pieces of jewelry, too.

## Daisy Chain

You may have made a daisy chain when you were a child. It is a simple beaded chain and one of the most commonly seen. It has a multitude of variations. Use different colors and sizes of beads, as well as the different weaves, to get your own special effect. Graphics and instructions are provided here for several variations of the daisy stitch.

### MATERIALS FOR PRACTICING

80 "color 1" 8° seed beads

80 "color 2" 8° seed beads

18 to 20 6° seed beads

Nymo 4, Silamide or similar thread

Size 10 or 12 beading needle

Scissors

**Single Daisy (Open)**

1. Single-thread the needle with as much thread as you feel comfortable with.

2. Choose one color of 8° seed beads for the flower (color 1) and another for the connector beads (color 2). The 6° seed beads are for the flower centers.

3. Tie a waste bead on the thread, leaving an 8" tail to add a clasp later if desired.

4. Thread on five color 2 beads and eight color 1 beads and pass thread back through the first of the color 1 beads picked up (Figure 2-28).

FIGURE 2-28    FIGURE 2-29    FIGURE 2-30

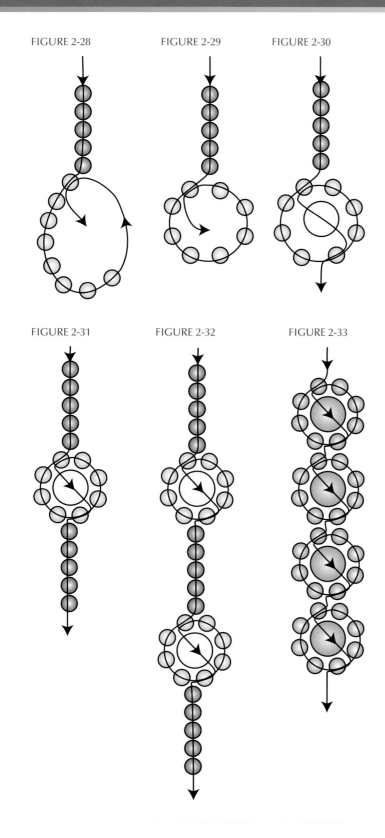

FIGURE 2-31    FIGURE 2-32    FIGURE 2-33

5. Pull up beads snugly so you have a ring at the end of the connector beads (Figure 2-29). Keep beads tight together as you work because you can't tighten them later.

6. Thread on one 6° bead. Pass needle across circle of beads and go through the one directly opposite where you just exited. Take needle from right to left through this bead and pull snugly (Figure 2-30).

7. Thread on five more color 2 beads (Figure 2-31).

8. Repeat from step 4 until you have the desired length (Figure 2-32).

## Single Daisy (Closed)

The flower in the closed daisy is made the same way as in the single daisy. Instead of picking up connector beads between flowers, you just make another flower. The chain is one flower after another. You can alternate colors or do it all the same color. Figure 2-33 shows how it is woven.

1. Single-thread your needle with as much thread as you feel comfortable with.

2. Choose one color of bead for each flower (colors 1 and 2). The 6° is the center bead.

3. Tie a waste bead on your thread, leaving an 8" tail so you can add a clasp later if desired.

4. Thread on eight color 1 8° seed beads and pass thread back through the first one of the color 1 beads picked up (Figure 2-33).

5. Thread on one 6° bead and pass back through the fifth bead of the first eight 8° beads picked up (Figure 2-33).

6. Pick up eight color 2 8° beads and pass back through the first one picked up.

7. Repeat step 5.

8. Continue repeating steps 4 through 7 until you have the length desired.

## Double Daisy

FIGURE 2-34

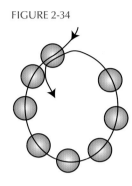

Instructions are given for the red, clear and black bracelet.

**1.** Single-thread the needle with as much thread as you feel comfortable with.

**2.** Tie a waste bead on the thread, leaving an 8" tail for a clasp to be added later if desired.

**3.** Thread on eight red beads and pass back through the first bead (Figure 2-34).

**4.** Pull them into a ring (Figure 2-35).

**5.** Thread on a black bead and pass the needle through lower left bead of the first ring of eight beads (Figure 2-36).

**6.** Thread on a clear bead and pass the needle back through the lower right bead of the first flower.

**7.** Thread on one clear bead and pass the needle back through the first clear bead you added (Figure 2-37).

**8.** Thread on six clear beads and pass the needle through the upper right bead on the clear flower (second one you added).

**9.** Thread on a black bead and pass the needle through the lower left clear bead (Figure 2-38).

**10.** Continue weaving in this manner until you have the desired length.

FIGURE 2-35

FIGURE 2-38

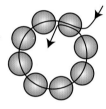

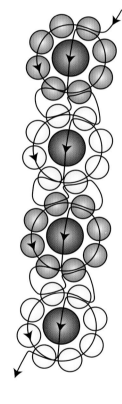

FIGURE 2-36

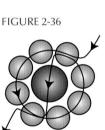

FIGURE 2-37

# Ladder Stitch

The bracelets in the accompanying photo were all done in ladder stitch. It's a stitch that works very well with bugle beads, as they lay side-by-side so well. It is also effective when done in seed beads because you can incorporate a pattern. Ladder stitch is one of the stitches used to make beaded flowers and animals.

Ladder stitch is most often used in conjunction with other stitches. It is frequently used as a base for brick stitch and vertical netting.

Ladder stitch is usually done with one thread. Since I didn't know this when I started, my knowledge of double-needle right-angle weave followed with me, and I started making ladders with two needles. It made sense to me to do them that way. Just so I don't offend the traditionalists out there, I will give the graphs for the traditional way to do ladder stitch and my version.

## Single-Needle Ladder Stitch

**1.** Single-thread the needle and string on two beads. Tie the thread in a knot so the beads sit side by side.

**2.** Pass the needle through the second bead, string on a third bead, pass the needle back through the second bead and then through the third (Figures 2-39 and 2-40).

**3.** String on a fourth bead, pass back through the third and then pass through the fourth. Continue in this manner until you reach the desired length (Figure 2-41). Note: You can combine bead types, like seed beads with bugle beads for another option (Figure 2-42).

## Double-Needle Ladder Stitch

**1.** Place a needle on each end of the thread, string two beads on one needle and pass the second needle through the last bead from the opposite direction.

**2.** String a third bead on one needle and pass the second needle through it from the opposite direction (Figures 2-43 and 2-44). Note: The thread is shown in two colors in the illustration so you can see how the thread passes back and forth through the beads.

**3.** Continue in this manner until you reach the desired length (Figure 2-45). Note: Again, a different look can be accomplished by combining beads (Figure 2-46).

FIGURE 2-39

FIGURE 2-40

The same ladder stitch as Figure 3-39, only this time done with bugle beads.

FIGURE 2-41

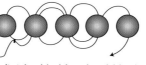

A finished ladder should look like this, except that the beads should be tight side-by-side.

FIGURE 2-42

Shows how a combination of bugle and seed beads should look when the thread has passed through.

FIGURE 2-43

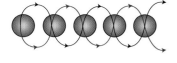

FIGURE 2-44

Shows the same thing as Figure 2-43, but done with bugle beads.

FIGURE 2-45

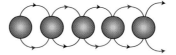

Shows how the ladder should look after the thread passes through, except that the beads should be tight side-by-side.

FIGURE 2-46

The pattern works the same no matter how many beads in the ladder. Just remember to pull the beads so they sit side-by-side.

# Spiral Rope

This stitch makes a lovely, yet durable, round rope because the thread passes through every core bead at least three times. Use beads with large holes, such as Japanese seed beads or slightly larger beads. This stitch can be done with a variety of bead sizes, each of which gives it a totally different look, as shown in the accompanying photo.

The instructions given here are for the basic stitch, using the same size beads. It is easier to learn if you use just two colors of beads. The illustrations show each bunch of three beads in a different color just so it is easier to differentiate each pass-through and how the beads fall into place as you weave. Use 8° seed beads to practice with.

**1.** Single-thread the needle and choose a color to be the core bead (the one that goes through the middle). It is not necessary to add a stop bead, as you will pass back through the beads in the first pass-through.

**2.** String on four of the core beads and three of the outside beads (Figure 2-47).

**3.** Pass back through the four core beads (Figure 2-48) and pull the thread snugly. Push the core beads to the left. (Reverse this process if left-handed.)

**4.** String on one core bead and three outside beads (Figure 2-49).

**5.** Skip the first core bead and pass thread through the next three core beads from the bottom up. Then pass through the core bead you just added (Figure 2-50). Push the outside beads to the left.

**6.** String on one core bead and three outside beads (Figure 2-51).

**7.** Skip the bottom two core beads and pass back through the next three beads and the core bead you just picked up (Figure 2-52). Pull the thread snugly and push the outside beads to the left. Continue in this manner until the rope is as long as desired.

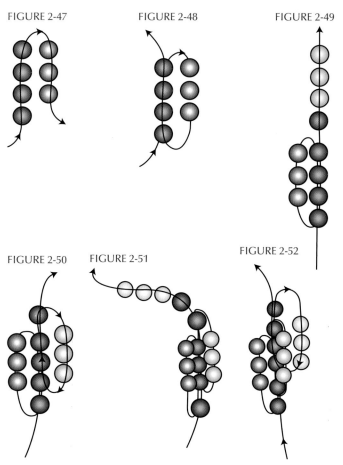

FIGURE 2-47      FIGURE 2-48      FIGURE 2-49

FIGURE 2-50      FIGURE 2-51      FIGURE 2-52

## Lacy Spiral

This lacy spiral design is a variation of a Dutch spiral weave and the brainchild of national beading instructor Cheryl Erickson. She has graciously allowed me to include her instructions here for all of you to enjoy. (Read more about Cheryl in the biography section at the back of the book.)

This spiral makes a lovely bracelet as you can see in the photo. You can vary it greatly, depending on the beads and colors used. You can make it tight or lacy, depending on the number of the smallest beads used.

### MATERIALS FOR PRACTICING

600 to 700 14° or 15° seed beads

140 to 160 11° seed beads

70 to 80 8° seed beads

70 to 80 5° or 6° seed beads

Nymo D thread

Size 10 or 12 beading needle

Scissors

Bead sorting dish or cloth

### Practice

1. Single-thread the needle.

2. Row 1: String on one 6° bead, one 8°, one 11° and one 14°, leaving a 6" tail.

3. Pass the needle through all of the beads again to form a circle, bringing the needle out through the 6° bead (Figure 2-53).

4. Row 2: Add one 8° bead and bring the needle through the previous 8° bead (Figure 2-54).

5. Add one 11° bead and bring the needle through the previous 11° bead (Figure 2-55).

6. Add two 14° beads and one 6° bead and bring the needle through the 6° bead in the previous row (Figure 2-56).

7. Row 3: Repeat steps 4 through 6 from row 2, except in step 6, add three 14° beads instead of two.

8. Rows 4 through 7: Repeat steps 4 through 6 from row 2, but continue increasing the number of 14° beads by one for each row until you reach seven 14° beads in row 7.

9. Remaining rows: Continue adding rows using seven 14° beads until you are 1¼" from the desired finished length. Then, decrease the 14° beads by one in each row until you are down to one.

FIGURE 2-53    FIGURE 2-54    FIGURE 2-55    FIGURE 2-56

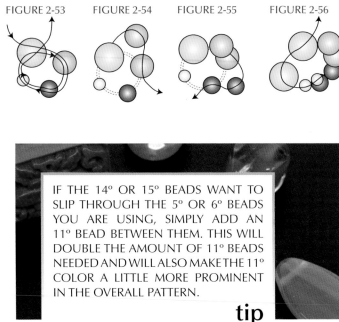

IF THE 14° OR 15° BEADS WANT TO SLIP THROUGH THE 5° OR 6° BEADS YOU ARE USING, SIMPLY ADD AN 11° BEAD BETWEEN THEM. THIS WILL DOUBLE THE AMOUNT OF 11° BEADS NEEDED AND WILL ALSO MAKE THE 11° COLOR A LITTLE MORE PROMINENT IN THE OVERALL PATTERN.

tip

# Potawatomi Weave

My friend, Donnie Cripe, works at Hardies Beads in Quartzsite, Ariz. I admired a necklace she was wearing made in Potawatomi weave and she gave me some instructions on how to do it. It is a weave comprised of three beads on top of two beads. Use 8° seed beads or 4mm round beads to practice this stitch.

1. Single-thread the needle and start with two colors of the same size bead—in this case, orange and blue.

2. String on two orange beads, one blue, one orange and one blue bead. Take them to within 6" of the end of the thread and tie them into a circle with a double-knot (Figure 2-57). Be sure to keep the working thread to the left.

3. Hold the ring of beads with your left thumb and forefinger so your fingers just cover the two orange beads. (Use opposite hand if you are left-handed.) Thread on one blue, one orange, one blue, one orange and one blue bead (Figure 2-58).

4. Pass the needle through the orange bead between the two blue ones in the first ring and through the first orange bead you picked up in the second pickup (Figure 2-59). Note the direction the needle passes through the second orange bead. You are actually passing through the second orange bead in the opposite direction than you did on the first pass.

5. Pull the thread up snugly until the three blue beads fall into a line above the two orange beads (Figure 2-60).

6. Work your thumb and forefinger up the piece as you complete each row, keeping the thread tight. String on one blue, one orange, one blue, one orange and one blue bead. Pass through the orange bead between the two blue ones in the second ring and through the first orange bead in the third pickup (Figure 2-61) and pull snugly.

7. Continue working in this manner until you have the length you want, with the finished stitch looking like that shown (Figure 2-62).

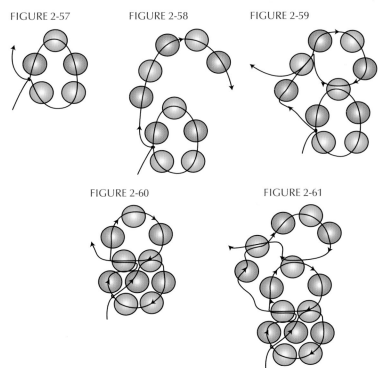

FIGURE 2-57

FIGURE 2-58

FIGURE 2-59

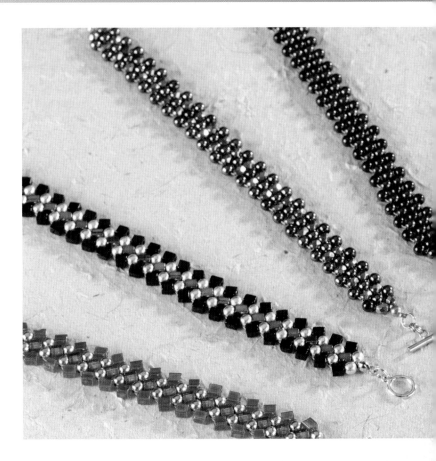

FIGURE 2-60

FIGURE 2-61

FIGURE 2-62

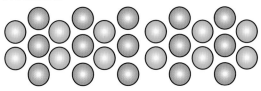

# USING WEAVING STITCHES

This section focuses on weaving stitches that can be used in many ways. Because this is a beginner's guide, only the most basic use of the stitch is included. Each of these stitches has enough uses and variations to fill a book of its own and many have been written. If you enjoy a particular stitch, buy a book or take a class on that stitch and learn all about it.

## Right-Angle Weave

There are two ways to do right-angle weave: with one needle or with two. Either one results in the same look. Try both methods and choose the one you prefer.

Right-angle weave is composed of patterns of four beads. These patterns are called squares. If you use bugle beads or other straight beads, the pattern does make a square. If you use round beads, however, the pattern will look more like a diamond.

Right-angle weave does not work well with all beads. Bugles, rounds, ovals and bicones generally work the best. If you are unsure, try the beads to see if they will work.

### Double-Needle Right-Angle Weave

1. Place a needle on each end of the thread, being sure to keep the thread in the needles even in length.

2. String four beads on one needle and center them on the thread.

3. Pass the second needle through the last bead you picked up from the opposite direction and pull up snugly to form a square- or diamond-shape centered on the thread (Figure 2-63). You can use more than one bead per side, but the pattern in regular right-angle weave will always have four sides.

4. String two beads on one needle and one on the second needle. Pass the second needle through the last bead on the first needle and pull up snugly, creating two squares (Figure 2-64).

5. Continue in this manner until you have the desired length. You are continuously doing a figure-eight pattern with the two needles.

### Single-Needle Right-Angle Weave

1. Cut a length of thread and single-thread the needle.

2. String on four beads and tie them together in a square knot between beads one and four, close to the end of the thread (Figure 2-65). Be careful not to tie them too tightly as you need a little wiggle room.

FIGURE 2-63   FIGURE 2-64

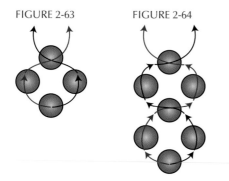

FIGURE 2-65    FIGURE 2-66

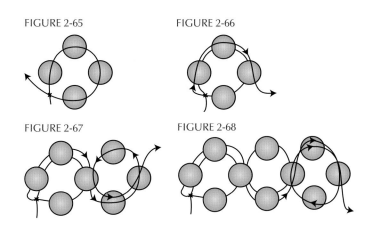

FIGURE 2-67    FIGURE 2-68

**3.** Pass the needle and thread back through beads 1, 2 and 3 (Figure 2-66).

**4.** String on three more beads (5, 6 and 7).

**5.** Pass back through bead 3 of the first square and then through beads 5 and 6 in the second square (Figure 2-67).

**6.** String on three more beads (8, 9 and 10) and pass back through bead 6, 8 and 9 (Figure 2-68).

**7.** Continue picking up three beads for each new square until you have the desired length.

## Right-Angle Weave Variations

The illustrations shown here, along with the variations in the photo, are meant to give you ideas of how you can change the basic stitch to achieve a look you like to make a necklace or bracelet strap. All of the variations shown can be done in either method. The list of possibilities is endless. Experiment and enjoy!

FIGURE 2-69

This variation is achieved by using the same size seed beads in two colors, placing the contrast color in the center of each weave pattern.

FIGURE 2-70

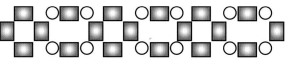

Use seed beads in one color and cube beads in another color to accomplish this variation.

FIGURE 2-71

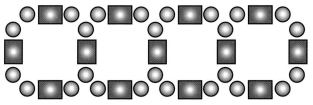

This variation also uses seed beads in one color and the cube beads in another, but instead of just one seed bead between each cube bead, there are two.

FIGURE 2-72

Use same-sized seed beads in two contrasting colors along with a bicone bead in a third color centered between stitch repeats.

FIGURE 2-73

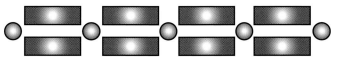

Bugle beads in one color and seed beads in another work together in this variation.

FIGURE 2-74

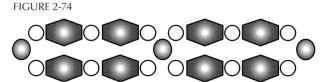

This option is created with seed beads in two different sizes and colors as well as barrel beads in yet another color.

FIGURE 2-75

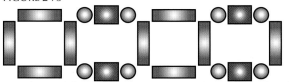

Use three different beads (bugle, seed and cube beads) in two different colors for this unique chain. Note how one repeat is made of bugles only, while the second repeat utilizes all three bead types.

FIGURE 2-76

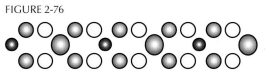

Even a weave in all round beads can become interesting when sizes and colors are varied as in this example.

FIGURE 2-77: Here is how the peyote pattern works up.

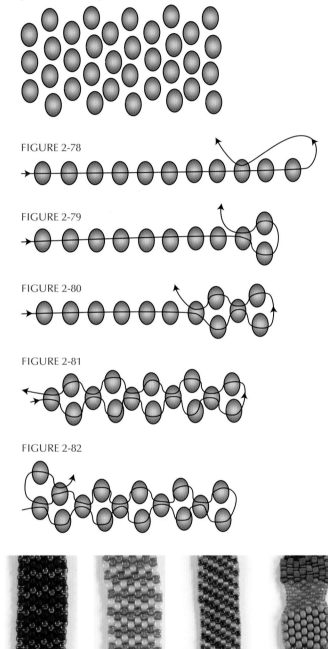

FIGURE 2-78

FIGURE 2-79

FIGURE 2-80

FIGURE 2-81

FIGURE 2-82

THESE FOUR BRACELETS ARE ALL DONE IN AN EIGHT-BEAD PATTERN. THE BLACK AND PINK ONES ALTERNATE TWO ROWS OF DARK BEADS WITH TWO ROWS OF LIGHT. THE GREEN BRACELET IS DONE BY ALTERNATING TWO COLORS OF BEADS IN THE SAME ROW. THIS RESULTS IN A DIAGONAL PATTERN. THE LAST BRACELET IS DONE USING DIFFERENT SIZES AND SHAPES OF BEADS. IT HAS THE SAME NUMBER OF BEADS IN EACH ROW.

# Peyote Stitch (Gourd Stitch)

This stitch has been around for hundreds of years and has several names: diagonal, twill, gourd and peyote to name a few. Gourd stitch and peyote are the most common terms. The term peyote is used by Native Americans to describe beadwork done with this stitch for religious and ceremonial purposes. The term peyote seems to be the most common contemporary name for this stitch.

There are a number of variations in peyote stitch, but most of the projects in this book that use peyote are done with the basic stitch. It is an extremely useful stitch in bead-setting cabochons.

The beads in peyote stitch are offset like paving bricks. They are stacked on each other in columns vertically as you make the rows horizontally. Because the beads are offset by half of a bead, it is easier to count the rows on a diagonal.

## Basic Even-Number Flat Peyote

1. Single-thread the needle and tie a stop bead within 4" of the end of the thread.

2. Thread on 11 same-sized beads (Figure 2-78). These beads will count as the first two rows of the piece.

3. Pass the thread through the third bead from the needle end, holding the third bead as you pass through it (Figure 2-78).

4. Pull the thread all the way through so the first bead is resting on the second bead (Figure 2-79). You may have to move it into position.

5. Thread on another bead with the needle and pass through the fifth bead (Figure 2-80).

6. Continue in this manner until you get to the end of the row (Figure 2-81). Push each set of two beads together to tighten the work. You may remove the stop bead at this time and tie the two threads in a knot or leave the threads and work the tail in later. *Note:* Your piece now has an up-and-down appearance. The beads that stick up are called "up-beads."

7. String on a new bead and pass through the second bead from the end, which is an up-bead (Figure 2-82).

8. String on another bead and pass through the next up-bead. Continue like this to the end of the row and continue adding beads and rows in this manner until you have the desired length.

# Vertical Netting (Lattice Weave)

Vertical netting is a versatile and useful weave, particularly when using found objects. It covers objects nicely, especially round objects, because it can expand and contract very well to fit a shape.

Vertical netting makes a bead fabric that resembles a net with diamond-shaped holes. It is built by going up and down the piece vertically. The diamond hole sizes vary according to how many beads are in each section. Always use an odd number of sections because the diamonds fit together in an offset pattern. The pattern will not work with an even number of sections.

## Basic Vertical Netting

**1.** Single-thread the needle and tie one "A" bead on the end in a single overhand knot so you can remove it easily later.

**2.** String on one "B" bead, two "A" beads, one "B," repeating the pattern until you have five sections of the two "A" beads. End with a one "B" and one "A." The completed pattern (Figure 2-83) should be: A-B-A-A-B-A-A-B-A-A-B-A-A-B-A-A-B-A.

**3.** Skip the last "A" bead you threaded on and pass back through the last "B" bead. (Be sure the beads in the first row are snug together at this point.)

**4.** String on two "A" beads, one "B" bead and two "A" beads and pass the needle through the third "B" bead from the bottom (Figure 2-84).

**5.** Repeat A-A-B-A-A pattern again, pass through the fifth "B" bead from the bottom, and end row with A-A-B-A pattern.

**6.** Repeat steps 3 through 5 for each additional row (Figure 2-85).

FIGURE 2-83          FIGURE 2-84          FIGURE 2-85

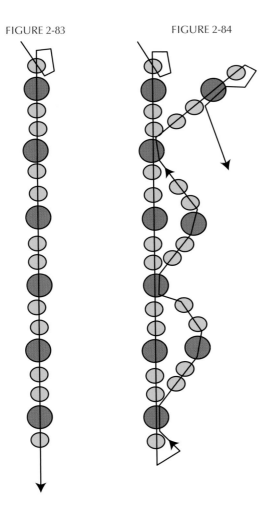

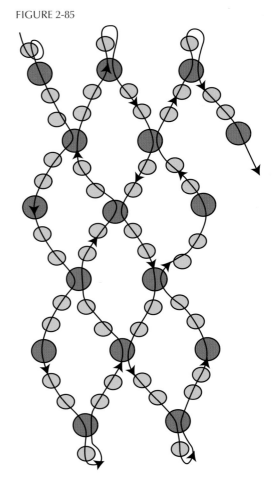

THIS WINE BOTTLE COVER PROJECT, WHICH IS DETAILED ON PAGES 122 THROUGH 124, IS A BEAUTIFUL EXAMPLE OF A TUBE STITCHED IN VERTICAL NETTING.

## Vertical Netting Tube

**1.** Bring the ends of a flat netting piece around to meet. Come out of the left bottom point "A" bead and pass through the "B" bead.

**2.** String on two "A" beads and immediately swing over to the next "B" bead on the right and pass through it.

**3.** String on two more "A" beads and pass through the "B" bead on the left.

**4.** Keep going back and forth across and up the piece (Figure 2-86), lacing it together until you get to the original "A" bead you tied on the end of the thread in the beginning.

**5.** Either untie the half-knot and work the two threads through the piece to end, or leave the knot around the bead and tie the two thread ends together and then work them back through the piece and tie them off. You can then run a thread through all the point beads to gather it to fit whatever object you want.

FIGURE 2-86

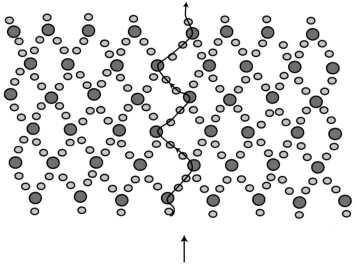

YOU WILL BE CREATING POINTS AT THE TOPS AND BOTTOMS OF THE PIECE. THIS IS HOW YOU COUNT THE NUMBER OF ROWS YOU NEED TO COVER SOMETHING. FOR EXAMPLE, IF YOU NEED 20 ROWS TO GO AROUND AN ITEM, YOU WOULD WORK THE PIECE UNTIL YOU HAD 20 POINTS TOP AND BOTTOM. KEEP IN MIND THAT THE BEGINNING HALF-POINT AND THE ENDING HALF-POINT ARE INCLUDED IN THAT NUMBER. WHEN YOU JOIN THE ENDS THOSE POINTS WILL WORK INTO THE PIECE.

tip

# Square Stitch

Square stitch is one of my favorite stitches. It looks just like loom weaving when it's finished, but you don't have all those warp threads to deal with. It is slower than loom weaving because you add beads one at a time. You can do two or three at a time, but I don't personally care for how the finished weaving looks, so I seldom use that method. Use the same size beads to do this stitch while you're learning; 8° beads are always a good practice size.

**1.** Single-thread the needle and tie a stop bead within a few inches of the end.

**2.** Thread five beads on the needle (Figure 2-87) and take them to the end of the thread.

**3.** Thread on one bead (Figure 2-88) and pass thread back through the last bead of the five you just picked up.

**4.** Pass the thread through the sixth bead again and pull up snugly until the sixth bead sits on the fifth bead (Figure 2-89).

**5.** Thread on the seventh bead, pass thread into the fourth bead and back up and through the seventh bead. Continue across the row in this manner (Figure 2-90).

**6.** Turn the corner by picking up the 11th bead. Pass thread through the 10th bead and back through the 11th bead (Figure 2-91).

**7.** Continue weaving back and forth across the row in this manner until you have the length you want.

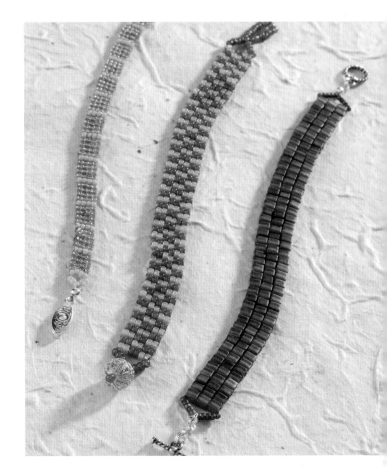

FIGURE 2-87

FIGURE 2-88

FIGURE 2-89

FIGURE 2-90

FIGURE 2-91

CLOSE-UP OF THE WEAVE USING 11° SEED BEADS (UPPER LEFT), 8° SEED BEADS (ABOVE) AND CUBE BEADS (LEFT).

# DESIGN PRINCIPLES AND COLOR THEORY

As you work, keep in mind the intended use of your finished design. Length, size and weight of beads, usage (formal or casual), ease of wearing and the personality for whom you are designing are all considerations you need to ponder before starting. Match your materials to your design. This will become easier with practice. Making jewelry is a very personal experience. Your personality, creativity and taste will greatly impact your designs. If you are designing an original pattern, there are a few principles of design that you might want to keep in mind. These principles will help give your designs that polished look.

# SYMMETRICAL PATTERNS

Symmetrical designs are the same on both sides of the piece. Usually, you will have a focal point in the middle of the design and then each side is a mirror image of the other. Be sure your patterns are exactly the same on either side of the focal point, as small variations show up as glaring errors in a symmetrical design.

# ASYMMETRICAL PATTERNS

Each side of an asymmetrical design is not a mirror image of the other. Instead, the main focal point is put off to one side. The weight of the off-center focal point will have to be counterbalanced on the other side of the piece, or the weight of the focal point will pull it to the center of the piece as it is worn.

Balance can be achieved in a variety of ways. Use numerous beads, strands or heavy beads to counter the weight of the focal point.

THIS BROOCH, WHICH APPEARED IN *BEADED JEWELRY WITH FOUND OBJECTS* (KP BOOKS, 2004), IS AN ASYMMETRICAL DESIGN. THE FRINGE IS OFF TO ONE SIDE. THE WEIGHT OF THE PIECE IS BALANCED BY THE PIN BACKING.

THIS JADE NECKLACE IS A PERFECT EXAMPLE OF A SYMMETRICAL DESIGN.

# RANDOM PATTERNS

A random design does not have a formal structure. It is spontaneous and usually without discernible pattern.

Even a random design needs some thought, though. Use beads, colors and materials that work well together. Choosing a color range or a theme will give the piece continuity, while the randomness of the construction will give it spontaneity.

# REPEATING PATTERNS

Repeating patterns usually consist of a number of beads placed in a particular order or pattern. That pattern is then duplicated over and over until you reach the length you need. Sometimes, two or more patterns are alternated to give variety and spice to a design. Repeating patterns are often used in symmetrical designs.

THIS NECKLACE IS AN EXAMPLE OF A RANDOM DESIGN. THREE STRANDS OF VARYING LENGTH SHOWCASE A VARIETY OF BEADS IN A BLUE-AND-GREEN COLOR SCHEME. THE STRANDS ARE GATHERED INTO ONE STRAND ON EITHER END AND THE NECKLACE IS FINISHED IN A SIMPLE PATTERN.

THIS EYEGLASS HOLDER IS A PERFECT EXAMPLE OF A REPEATING PATTERN. THERE IS A BASIC SIX-BEAD PATTERN THAT IS REPEATED THROUGHOUT THE LENGTH OF THE PIECE. THE LIGHT AND DARK ASPECT OF THIS COLOR SCHEME MAKES IT APPEAR AS THOUGH THERE ARE ACTUALLY ALTERNATING LIGHT AND DARK PATTERNS.

# COLOR THEORY

Another area that people often need help in is color theory. Hundreds of books have been written on the subject of color theory—even some on color theory and beading. If you have not had the benefit of a good class on color theory, you will find the purchase of such a book useful. Because the subject is so vast, only the highlights are presented here.

In traditional pigment-based color theory, the three primary colors are red, yellow and blue (Figure 3-2). These colors are primary because they are pure color and can't be mixed from other colors.

The secondary colors are a combination mixed from the primary colors (Figure 3-3). Red and yellow make orange. Yellow and blue make green. Blue and red make purple.

So the basic color wheel consists of red, orange, yellow, green, blue and purple.

The color wheel is further expanded when these colors are mixed with the ones on either side of them, resulting in tertiary colors like blue-green, red-orange and yellow-green (Figure 3-4).

The color wheel is true in theory though not in fact because all sorts of things influence color. However, we can use the basic color wheel for a general guide when choosing color schemes for beads. Remember, though, that beads are often reflective and the way light hits them greatly affects their color. The best way to choose beads is to lay them out next to each other to see how they work together.

Color is a very personal matter and those colors that work best for you are the ones that you like the best. If you are having trouble choosing colors, though, the following color schemes can be used as a guide for choosing beads for your projects.

## Monochromatic

Monochromatic color schemes consist of one color. Using different shades, tints, tones or hues of a single color can result in a harmonious blend that will produce a rich color experience.

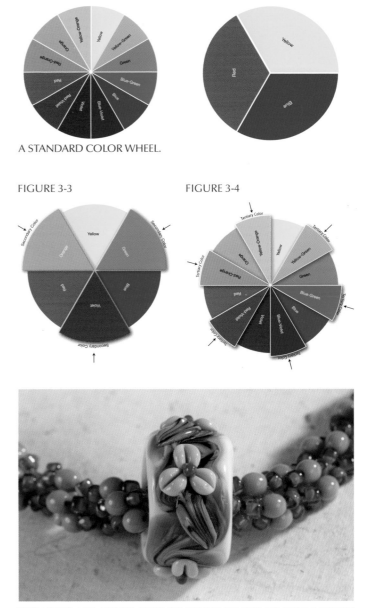

FIGURE 3-1

FIGURE 3-2

A STANDARD COLOR WHEEL.

FIGURE 3-3

FIGURE 3-4

THE NECKLACE ABOVE GETS ITS DEPTH OF COLOR FROM USING THREE SHADES OF TURQUOISE BEADS IN A MONOCHROMATIC COLOR SCHEME. THE SLIDER PROVIDED THE INSPIRATION FOR THE COLOR CHOICES.

# Complementary

Complementary colors lie directly opposite each other on the color wheel. The famous Christmas colors red and green are complementary colors, as are yellow and purple or blue and orange. These opposites enhance each other. Use of them together often makes each color appear more vibrant.

THE WHIMSICAL MULTI-STRAND BRACELET AT THE RIGHT, WHICH WAS FEATURED IN *BEADED JEWELRY WITH FOUND OBJECTS* (KP BOOKS, 2004), IS AN EXAMPLE OF A COMPLEMENTARY COLOR SCHEME BECAUSE IT IS MADE WITH RED AND GREEN BEADS. RED AND GREEN ARE DIRECTLY ACROSS FROM ONE ANOTHER ON A STANDARD COLOR WHEEL, AS SHOWN ON PAGE 43.

# Triad

A triad is a color scheme composed of three colors equidistant on the color wheel like red, yellow and blue, or green, orange and purple. They can be any three colors, but they have to form an equilateral triangle on the color wheel.

ALTHOUGH NOT PURE COLORS, THE BEADS ON THIS MEMORY WIRE BRACELET FORM A TRIAD COLOR SCHEME OF RED, YELLOW AND BLUE.

# Split Complementary

A split complementary color scheme gets a little more complicated. It consists of a color and the two colors on either side of its direct complement. You will need to balance the colors carefully in this color scheme.

THIS WOVEN BRACELET ISN'T A TRUE SPLIT COMPLIMENTARY COLOR SCHEME, BUT IT SHOWS THE GENERAL IDEA. THE LAVENDER (PURPLE) WOULD BE THE PRIMARY COLOR AND THE YELLOW-GREEN AND DARK YELLOW WOULD BE THE TWO COLORS ON EITHER SIDE OF PURPLE'S COMPLEMENT, YELLOW.

# Analogous

An analogous color scheme uses two or more colors that are adjacent to each other on the color wheel. Blue and green would be one example. Red, orange and yellow would be another. Colors adjacent to each other on the color wheel harmonize well, making them easy to use together.

THIS SQUARE-STITCHED BRACELET SEGMENT SHOWS IS A WONDERFUL EXAMPLE OF AN ANALOGOUS COLOR SCHEME CONSISTING OF BLUE, GREEN AND PURPLE.

# PROJECTS

Whenever you start a new craft, you really should start with the basics. It doesn't get much more basic in jewelry than a one-strand necklace on thread. Just because it's simple doesn't mean it can't be attractive. Once you've mastered the simple, move on to more challenging pieces: multiple-strand stringing; using multiple-hole beads; using head and eye pins; working with memory wire; beads and wirework; bead embroidery; simple cabochon beading; loom weaving; making woven chains; and weaving stitches. It's all represented in the array of projects that follow, so enjoy!

## MATERIALS

- 96 gold-plated 11º seed beads (A)
- 72 white 6mm freshwater pearls (B)
- 26 red 6mm flat faceted disk beads (C)
- 13 purple 10mm faceted hex-cut beads (D)
- Small gold toggle clasp
- 4 gold clamshell bead tips
- 1 pair gold earring findings
- 3 gold 5mm split rings
- 4 gold 2mm crimp beads
- 84" white Beadalon® DandyLine™ .006"-diameter thread
- Size 12 beading needle
- Jewelry glue
- Bead sorting dish or cloth
- Round nose pliers
- Split ring pliers
- Scissors
- Tape measure

## SIMPLE ONE-STRAND STRINGING

### BEAD KEY

○    11º gold-plated seed beads (A)

◯    6mm white freshwater pearls (B)

⬭    6mm red flat faceted disk beads (C)

    10mm purple faceted hex-cut beads (D)

# PURPLE AND PEARLS JEWELRY SET

This set was made with members of a social group prone to wearing hats in mind. To make the project yours, choose beads and colors that suit your taste. In a simple project like this, the beads become very important, so choose carefully.

# MAKING THE NECKLACE

**1.** Cut 60" of thread and double-thread the needle.

**2.** Tie a crimp bead securely on the very end of the thread with several overhand knots. Glue the knots and trim excess thread.

FIGURE 4-1

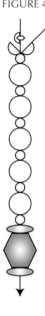

**3.** Pass the needle through one clamshell bead tip from the inside out. Close the jaws of the clamshell around the knot with pliers, as in Option 4 on page 20.

**4.** Place the beads in a sorting dish or on a cloth.

**5.** Refer to the Bead Key and thread on beads in the following sequence (Figure 4-1): A-B-A-B-A-B-A-B-A-B-A-C-D-C.

**6.** Repeat step 5 (Figure 4-1) 10 more times.

**7.** Finish the strand with bead sequence A-B-A-B-A-B-A-B-A-B-A.

**8.** Thread on one clamshell bead tip from the bottom up and push down the thread against the beads.

**9.** Clip one strand of the doubled thread about 1" down from needle.

**10.** Thread a crimp bead on the needle with a single thread and push it into the bowl of the clamshell.

**11.** Use both threads to tie off the thread and knot it against the crimp bead. Glue the knot, trim the thread ends and close the clamshell around the knot.

**12.** Spread a split ring with split ring pliers and insert it into the hole on the loop end of the toggle clasp. Turn the ring through the loop until it is on completely.

**13.** Bend the bar of the clamshell at one end of the necklace around the split ring with round nose pliers.

**14.** Attach a split ring to the bar end of the toggle as in step 13 and then thread another split ring onto the first for the finished look shown. (You need the additional length so the bar end of the toggle has enough room to bend through the loop.)

STEP 14: THE FINISHED ENDS OF THE NECKLACE.

47

# MAKING THE EARRINGS

**1.** Cut 12" of thread and double-thread the needle. Tie a crimp bead about 2" from end of the thread. Pass through a clamshell bead tip from inside. Don't close it.

**2.** Refer to the Bead Key on page 46 and thread on beads in the following sequence (Figure 4-2): A-A-B-A-B-A-B-A-C-A-D-A-C-A-B-A-B-A-B-A-A.

**3.** Pass the needle and thread through the clamshell and the crimp bead.

**4.** Tie off the threads against the crimp bead. Glue the knot and trim the excess threads.

**5.** Close the clamshell with pliers.

**6.** Bend the bar of the clamshell through the loop on the earring finding using round nose pliers for the finished look shown at right.

**7.** Repeat steps 1 through 6 for the second earring.

STEP 6: CLOSE-UP OF ONE FINISHED EARRING.

FIGURE 4-2

THESE BASIC INSTRUCTIONS WILL WORK FOR A BRACELET AS WELL. JUST STRING BEADS IN THE CORRECT LENGTH TO GO AROUND YOUR WRIST. WHEN MEASURING, REMEMBER TO ALLOW ¾" TO 1" FOR THE CLASP.

**tip**

## MATERIALS (FOR BLACK AND PEARL STRAND)

- 34 gold-plated 11° seed beads (A)
- 32 white 6mm freshwater pearls (B)
- 30 gold 4mm flat spacer beads (C)
- 8 gold 10mm filigree beads (D)
- 14 black 10mm x 7mm faceted vertically drilled teardrop beads (E)
- 7 gold-washed black 17mm x 10mm beads (F)
- 1 pair gold eyeglass holders
- 26" bright Beadalon® 49-strand .018"-diameter stringing wire
- 2 #1 gold Beadalon® crimp beads
- 2 gold 5mm split rings
- Wire cutters
- Crimp pliers
- Split ring pliers
- Jewelry pliers
- Bead sorting dish or cloth
- Tape measure

### BEAD KEY

- ○ 11° gold-plated seed beads (A)
- ○ 6mm white freshwater pearls (B)
- ▭ 4mm gold flat spacer beads (C)
- ◯ 10mm gold filigree beads (D)
- ⬖ 10mm x 7mm black faceted vertically drilled teardrop beads (E)
- ▭ 17mm x 10mm gold-washed black beads (F)

## SIMPLE ONE-STRAND STRINGING

# ELEGANT EYEGLASS HOLDERS

These elegant eyeglass holders were all made in the same pattern using just six beads, although you would never guess that was the case at first glance. The difference in beads makes all the difference in the look of the finished piece. The instructions given are for the black and pearl strand. If you wish to use different beads, simply refer to the Bead Key and replace the beads shown there with your choices. Then follow the stringing pattern. These strands are done on beading wire for durability. The main difference in using beading wire instead of thread is the way you secure the end of your strand. You need to use a crimp bead to hold wire.

## ATTACHING THE EYEGLASS HOLDER

**1.** Use the split ring pliers to attach a split ring to the loop of each eyeglass holder piece.

**2.** Cut 26" of wire.

**3.** Thread on one split ring-eyeglass holder piece and one crimp bead and take them to within ½" of the wire end.

**4.** Pass the wire end back through crimp bead, being sure to catch the split ring in the loop, and pull snugly.

**5.** Use crimp pliers to close and secure the crimp bead for an attached end, as shown at right.

STEP 5: THE EYEGLASS HOLDER IS ATTACHED TO THE END OF THE WIRE BEFORE BEADING THE STRAND.

## BEADING THE STRAND

FIGURE 4-3
Sequence
begins.

**1.** Thread on one gold 11° seed bead and one gold flat spacer bead, being sure to work wire end through beads.

**2.** Refer to the Bead Key on page 49 and thread on beads in the following sequence (Figure 4-3): B-A-B-A-D-A-B-A-B-C-E-C-F-C-E-C.

**3.** Repeat step 2 six more times.

**4.** End the strand with bead sequence B-A-B-A-D-A-B-A-B-C-A.

**Pearl & gold pattern.**

## FINISHING THE STRAND

**1.** Thread on one crimp bead and the remaining split ring-eyeglass holder piece.

**2.** Pass the wire end back through crimp bead, being sure to catch the split ring in the loop.

**3.** Continue to pass wire end through about ½" of the beaded strand and then pull wire snugly.

**4.** Use crimp pliers to close and secure the crimp bead.

**5.** Trim excess wire from the end.

PRACTICE USING THE CRIMPING TOOL ON SOME SCRAP PIECES OF WIRE BEFORE TRYING IT ON YOUR GOOD MATERIALS. HAVE THE CRIMP BEAD SNUG AGAINST THE SPLIT RING. REMEMBER TO USE THE 'W' SLOT FIRST TO CRIMP AROUND AND BETWEEN THE WIRES. THEN USE THE 'O' SLOT TO FOLD THE TWO SIDES TOGETHER.

**tip**

## MATERIALS (FOR 7" FRUIT BEAD BRACELET)

- 50 assorted fruit beads
- Wrist measurement plus 4" Beadalon® 031"-diameter Elasticity™
- Tape measure
- Scissors
- Pencil and scrap paper
- Bead sorting dish or cloth
- Gem-Tac™ or E-6000 glue (optional)

## MATERIALS (FOR 7" MEXICAN CUPS BRACELET)

- 50 assorted miniature cups
- Wrist measurement plus 4" Beadalon® 031"-diameter Elasticity™
- Tape measure
- Scissors
- Pencil and scrap paper
- Bead sorting dish or cloth
- Gem-Tac™ or E-6000 glue (optional)

## MATERIALS (FOR 7" BOULDER OPAL BEADS BRACELET)

- 25 black 18mm x 7mm two-holed beads
- 50 Boulder Opal 19mm x 8mm flat paddle glass beads
- 2 pieces (wrist measurement plus 4") Beadalon® 031"-diameter Elasticity™
- Tape measure
- Scissors
- Pencil and scrap paper
- Bead sorting dish or cloth
- Gem-Tac™ or E-6000 glue (optional)

## SIMPLE ONE-STRAND STRINGING

# FUN AND FUNKY ELASTIC BRACELETS

One of the easiest pieces of jewelry to make is an elastic bracelet. The only tool you need is a pair of scissors. Depending on the beads you choose, your bracelet can go from festive to funky, inexpensive to pricey. Here are three options.

# FRUIT BEAD BRACELET

These fruit beads are vintage German. The number of beads you will need for an elastic bracelet will depend on how big around your wrist is.

## INSTRUCTIONS

**1.** Measure your wrist, write the number down and add 4".

**2.** Cut elastic strand to the final length from step 1 (see Tip below).

**3.** Thread on the fruit beads randomly, as shown, testing the length around your wrist for size as you go. It should fit exactly, unless you prefer a looser fit. If so, add a few more beads.

**4.** Tie ends of elastic in a surgeon's knot, referring back to page 18 for detailed knotting instructions, if needed. Do not stretch the elastic that is inside the beads as you tie the knot. You need the stretch to be able to get it over your hand. Add a drop of glue to the knot for added durability, if desired.

**5.** Thread elastic ends back through the beaded strand on either side about ½" and trim ends with scissors.

STEP 3: DETAIL OF THE RANDOMLY BEADED STRAND.

IF YOU PREFER NOT TO WASTE THE ELASTIC, KEEP IT ON THE SPOOL AND DON'T CUT IT OFF UNTIL AFTER YOU HAVE THE BEADS THREADED ON. THIS WAY YOU USE ONLY WHAT YOU NEED.

**tip**

# MEXICAN CUPS BRACELET

Sometimes you find things that you can use in jewelry that aren't beads. Such is the case with this bracelet made with miniature ceramic cups. I found a string of these small cups as I was walking past a street vendor's booth in a small Mexican town. Look around you. You might be surprised what you can find that will make interesting jewelry.

## INSTRUCTIONS

**1.** Measure your wrist, write the number down and add 4".

**2.** Cut elastic strand to the final length from step 1 (see Tip from Fruit Bead Bracelet).

**3.** Thread on the miniature cups randomly, as shown, testing the length around your wrist for size as you go. It should fit exactly, unless you prefer a looser fit. If so, add a few more cups.

**4.** Tie ends of elastic in a surgeon's knot, referring back to page 18 for detailed knotting instructions, if needed. Do not stretch the elastic that is inside the beads as you tie the knot. You need the stretch to be able to get it over your hand. Add a drop of glue to the knot for added durability, if desired.

**5.** Trim elastic ends with scissors about ¼" from knot.

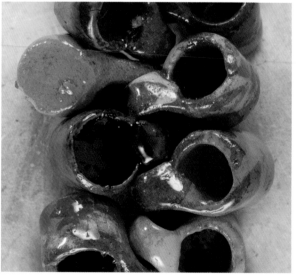

STEP 3: DETAIL OF THE RANDOMLY BEADED STRAND.

# BOULDER OPAL BEADS BRACELET

The glass paddle-shaped beads in this bracelet resemble the colors found in the matrix of Boulder Opals—those marvelous opals from Australia. Since I really like the opals, I certainly am a fan of the beads. Another favorite is any bead with two holes. Combining two favorites in a bracelet makes for a winning project.

## INSTRUCTIONS

**1.** Measure your wrist, write the number down and add 4".

**2.** Cut two elastic strands to the final length from step 1 (see Tip from Fruit Bead Bracelet, page 53).

**3.** Take one elastic strand and thread through one hole of a black bead followed by an opal bead.

**4.** Continue alternating black beads with opal beads until you have a strand long enough to encircle your wrist. Be sure to end with an opal bead.

**5.** Tie a loose knot in either end of the elastic to hold the beads in place.

**6.** Thread the other piece of elastic through the remaining hole in each black bead, adding an opal bead between each for the finished look shown.

**7.** Tie both ends of elastic in a surgeon's knot, referring back to page 18 for detailed knotting instructions, if needed. Do not stretch the elastic that is inside the beads as you tie the knot. You need the stretch to be able to get it over your hand. Also, you need to keep the elastic even in length so the bracelet doesn't buckle. Add a drop of glue to the knot for added durability, if desired.

**8.** Trim elastic ends with scissors close to the knots.

STEP 6: DETAIL OF FINISHED BEADED STRANDS SHOWING HOW THE BEADS LAY.

## MATERIALS (FOR 8½" PRETTY PEARLS BRACELET)

- 48 white 4mm freshwater pearls
- 48 pink 4mm freshwater pearls
- 48 beige 4mm freshwater pearls
- 3 Bali silver 10mm-diameter flower spacer beads
- 2 Bali silver 5mm round beads
- Silver toggle clasp
- 2 silver clamshell bead tips
- 2 silver 2mm crimp beads
- 5mm silver split ring
- 72" white Nymo D thread
- Size 12 beading needle
- Gem-Tac™ glue
- Round nose jewelry pliers
- Scissors
- Bead sorting dish or cloth
- Tape measure

# MULTI-STRAND BRACELETS

These three bracelets all use a single-strand clasp. Each one gets to that point in a different way.

# PRETTY PEARLS BRACELET

There are three shades of pearls in this bracelet. The multi-strand sections of this bracelet are divided by pretty Bali silver flower beads.

## BEADING THE MULTIPLE STRANDS

1. Cut 12" of thread and single-thread the needle.

2. Tie a crimp bead within 1" of the thread end with a double-knot.

3. Pass needle through clamshell bead tip from inside. Do not close clamshell.

4. Thread on one 5mm silver bead.

5. Thread on 12 white pearls and one flower bead.

6. Repeat step 5 twice more.

7. End strand with 12 white pearls and one 5mm silver bead.

8. Pass through a clamshell bead tip and remaining crimp bead.

9. Tie thread in a double-knot around crimp, being sure you have removed the slack from the thread.

10. Repeat step 1.

11. Pass thread through clamshell and the existing 5mm silver bead.

12. Repeat steps 5 through 9.

13. Repeat steps 10 and 11 twice, substituting the pink pearls for the white ones.

14. Repeat step 10 and 11 twice more, substituting the beige pearls for the white ones for the finished look shown below.

STEP 14: ALL SIX STRANDS COMPLETE.

## FINISHING THE BRACELET

1. Tie off knots securely, glue the knots and trim the thread ends.

2. Close clamshell around knots.

3. Attach a split ring to the bar end of the toggle clasp.

4. Use round nose pliers to bend the bar of the clamshell at one end of the bracelet around the split ring.

5. Bend the bar of the clamshell on the other end of the bracelet around loop end of toggle clasp for the finished clasp attachment shown at right.

STEP 5: ALL SIX STRANDS COME TOGETHER TO WORK WITH A SINGLE-STRAND TOGGLE CLASP.

This bracelet makes use of a three-hole strand spacer
at each end of the bracelet to keep strands separate.

## MATERIALS (FOR 8" BRACELET)

44 toffee-colored 6mm x 9mm rondelles • 20 topaz 8mm round beads • 46 gold 6mm square spacer beads

18 gold 3mm round beads • 2 gold 5mm round beads • 2 gold 4mm crimp beads • Gold toggle clasp

2 gold 5mm split rings • 2 gold Beadalon® three-hole strand spacers

27" bright Beadalon® 49-strand .018"-diameter stringing wire • Wire cutters

Crimp pliers • Split ring pliers • Tape • Bead sorting dish or cloth

## BEADING THE STRANDS

1. Cut three 9"-long pieces of wire.

2. Hold ends together and pass all three wire strands through one crimp bead, through the loop end of the toggle clasp and back through the crimp bead, leaving a ½" tail.

3. Use crimp pliers to close and secure the crimp bead.

4. Pass all wires, including ends, through a 5mm gold round bead.

5. Trim all three wire ends close to the 5mm gold round bead.

6. On one wire, thread on three 3mm gold round beads.

7. Pass wire through the outside hole of one three-hole strand spacer.

8. Alternate threading on one gold spacer with one toffee bead until you have 22 toffee beads. End sequence with one gold spacer.

9. Pass wire through the outside hole of the second three-hole spacer.

10. Thread on three 3mm gold round beads, a 5mm gold round bead and the remaining crimp bead.

11. Tape end of wire to prevent beads from slipping off.

12. Repeat steps 6 through 11 on other outside strand.

13. Thread on three 3mm gold round beads on remaining (center) strand and pass through the center hole of the strand spacer.

14. Thread on 20 topaz beads, for the three-strand look shown at right.

15. Pass wire through the remaining hole in second spacer and thread on three 3mm gold round beads.

16. Pass strand through 5mm gold round bead and the crimp bead.

17. Tape end of wire to prevent beads from slipping off.

STEP 14: THE TOPAZ STRAND LAYS BETWEEN THE IDENTICAL TWO OUTSIDE STRANDS.

# FINISHING THE BRACELET

1. Use split ring pliers to hook two split rings together and then attach one of those split rings through the bar end of the toggle clasp.

2. Remove tape from wires.

3. Pass all three wire ends through the end split ring, back through crimp bead and through the 5mm gold round bead. Pull wire snugly, but not tight.

4. Use crimp pliers to close and secure the crimp bead.

5. Trim ends close to 5mm gold round bead for the finished ends shown at right.

STEP 5: FINISHED ENDS OF THE BRACELET.

# COPPER FLASHES BRACELET

This bracelet has decorative findings at the end of it
that take the bracelet from three strands down to one.

## MATERIALS (FOR 8" BRACELET)

34 blue-and-copper 6mm x 9mm faceted rondelles • 19 copper-lined 5mm x 6mm bicones
36 copper 3mm round fluted beads • 20 copper 3mm round beads • 2 copper three-strand-to-one findings
Copper toggle clasp • 3 copper 4mm jump rings • 6 copper 2mm crimp beads
27" bright Beadalon® 49-strand .018"-diameter stringing wire • Wire cutters
Crimp pliers • Jewelry pliers • Tape • Bead sorting dish or cloth

## INSTRUCTIONS

**1.** Cut three 9"-long pieces of wire.

**2.** Pass one wire through a crimp bead, through one outside hole of one of the copper findings and back through the crimp bead for about ½".

**3.** Use crimp pliers to close and secure the crimp bead.

**4.** Alternate threading on one fluted 3mm copper round bead with one blue-and-copper rondelle until you have 17 rondelles. Finish strand with one fluted 3mm copper round bead.

**5.** Pass wire end through another crimp bead, through the other copper finding and back through the crimp bead. Pull up snugly, but not tight.

**6.** Use crimp pliers to close and secure the crimp bead.

**7.** Repeat steps 2 through 6 for the other outside strand.

**8.** Attach center strand wire as in steps 2 and 3.

**9.** Alternate threading on one 3mm copper round bead and one copper-lined bicone until you have 19 bicones. End with a 3mm copper round bead for the three-strand look shown at right.

STEP 9: THE PREDOMINANTLY COPPER CENTER STRAND LAYS
BETWEEN THE IDENTICAL BLUE-AND-COPPER OUTSIDE STRANDS.

**10.** Attach wire end to finding as in steps 5 and 6.

**11.** Attach one jump ring to loop end of the toggle clasp and to the hole on one finding.

**12.** Attach the other jump ring to the bar end of the toggle clasp and to the hole on the other finding for the finished ends shown at right.

STEP 12: THE DESIGN OF THE COPPER FINDING ALLOWS YOU TO EASILY ATTACH THREE BEADED STRANDS TO A SINGLE-STRAND TOGGLE CLASP.

SEVERAL COLORS OF BLUE CUBE AND SEED BEADS ARE LOOSELY BRAIDED TOGETHER IN THIS MULTI-STRAND NECKLACE TO HOLD A LAMPWORKED LOBSTER BEAD MADE BY SHARON PETERS. THE BEAD IS SUSPENDED FROM THE NECKLACE BY SEVERAL STRANDS OF BRANCHED FRINGE.

## MATERIALS

- 13 purple 12mm ammonite-shaped beads
- 13 purple 9mm offset bicones
- 11 purple 12mm twisted oval beads
- 74 gold 4mm fluted beads
- Gold toggle clasp
- 78 gold 2mm crimp beads
- 3 gold 5mm split rings
- 75" gold-plated Beadalon® 49-strand .018-diameter stringing wire
- Wire cutters
- Crimp pliers
- Split ring pliers
- Bead sorting dish or cloth
- Tape measure

## MULTI-STRAND STRINGING

# ILLUSION NECKLACE

Illusion necklaces have been around for some time. Usually, they are done on clear monofilament fishing line so the beads seem to float as you wear them. This necklace is done on gold-plated beading wire. Although the beads are the same color, the shapes are very different, adding interest to the necklace.

1. Cut three pieces of wire: 23", 25" and 27". *19, 21, 23 for 18"*

2. Start with 23" wire piece and thread on one crimp, one fluted bead, one twisted oval, one fluted bead and one crimp. Roughly center beads on wire.

3. Use the crimp pliers to close and secure the crimp bead at either end of the bead cluster for the look shown.

4. Move up the wire on either side about ⁷⁄₈" and repeat steps 2 and 3.

5. Continue adding bead clusters until you have five additional bead clusters up each side of wire roughly ⁷⁄₈" apart. Set strand aside.

6. Repeat steps 2 through 5 on the 25" piece of wire, substituting the bicones for the twisted oval beads, as shown below center. You will have a total of 13 bead clusters on this strand when finished. Set aside.

7. Repeat steps 2 through 5 on the 27" piece of wire, substituting the ammonite beads for the twisted oval beads, as shown below right. You will have a total of 13 bead clusters on this strand when finished. Set aside.

8. Attach one split ring to loop end of the toggle clasp and set aside.

9. Attach two split rings together and then attach one of those split rings to the bar end of the toggle clasp.

10. Gather the three strands together, thread two crimp beads on one end of the gathered strands, pass wire ends through a split ring on one end of the clasp and then pass wires back through the crimp beads for about ½".

11. Use crimp pliers to close and secure the crimp beads around the wires. Trim ends close to second crimp.

12. Repeat steps 10 and 11 for other end of the wire strands for the finished ends.

STEP 3: THE BEAD CLUSTER REPEATED ON THE SHORTEST STRAND.

STEP 6: THE BEAD CLUSTER REPEATED ON THE MIDDLE STRAND.

STEP 7: THE BEAD CLUSTER REPEATED ON THE REMAINING STRAND..

## MATERIALS

- 16 coral 12mm x 18mm two-hole domed beads (A)

- 55 turquoise 6mm drum-shaped beads (B)

- 44 Bali silver 6mm flat daisy spacer beads (C)

- 44 Bali silver 4mm x 6mm spacer beads (D)

- 4 silver 2.5mm round beads (E)

- 25mm x 26mm coral wedge-shaped pendant bead (F)

- Silver magnetic two-hole clasp

- 48" bright Beadalon® 49-strand .018"-diameter stringing wire

- 2mm silver crimp bead

- Wire cutter

- Jewelry pliers

- Crimp pliers

- Bead sorting dish or cloth

- Tape measure

## USING MULTIPLE-HOLE BEADS

## BEAD KEY

12mm x 18mm coral two-hole domed beads (A)

6mm turquoise drum-shaped beads (B)

6mm Bali silver flat daisy spacer beads (C)

4mm x 6mm Bali silver spacer beads (D)

2.5mm silver round beads (E)

25mm x 26mm coral wedge-shaped pendant (F)

# CORAL AND TURQUOISE NECKLACE

The two-hole coral beads featured in this necklace were originally part of an elastic bracelet. I took the bracelet apart and combined the beads with turquoise and Bali silver to make this necklace.

# BEADING THE STRANDS

1. Insert ends of 48" wire through holes in magnetic end of clasp and center the clasp on the wire, creating two wire strands.

2. Refer to the Bead Key and complete Pattern 1 (Figure 4-4) on both wire strands, which is the following bead sequence: C-B-D-B-C.

3. Pass each wire end through one hole of a coral bead (Figure 4-5). Remember to keep the domed side of the coral beads all facing up.

4. Complete Pattern 2 (Figure 4-6) on both wire strands, which is the following bead sequence: D-B-D.

5. Pass each wire end through one hole of a coral bead (Figure 4-7).

6. Repeat Pattern 1 (Figure 4-4) twice more, being sure to thread on a coral bead after each repeat.

7. Repeat Pattern 2 (Figure 4-6) and thread on a coral bead.

8. Repeat Pattern 1 (Figure 4-4) twice more, being sure to thread on a coral bead after each repeat.

9. Repeat Pattern 2 (Figure 4-6) and thread on a coral bead.

# ADDING THE PENDANT

1. Choose one wire for the top and thread the following bead sequence (Figure 4-8): E-E-B-E-E.

2. Thread onto the other wire strand in following bead sequence (Figure 4-8): C-B-C-F-C-B-C.

3. Pass each wire end through one hole of a coral bead, as shown below to complete the adding of the pendant to the piece.

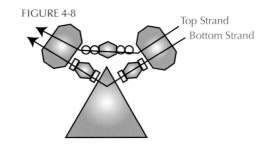

FIGURE 4-8

Top Strand
Bottom Strand

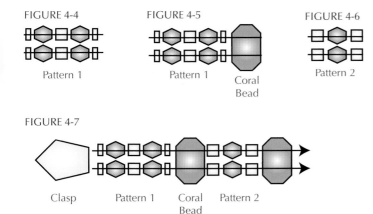

FIGURE 4-4

Pattern 1

FIGURE 4-5

Pattern 1          Coral
                   Bead

FIGURE 4-6

Pattern 2

FIGURE 4-7

Clasp      Pattern 1      Coral      Pattern 2
                          Bead

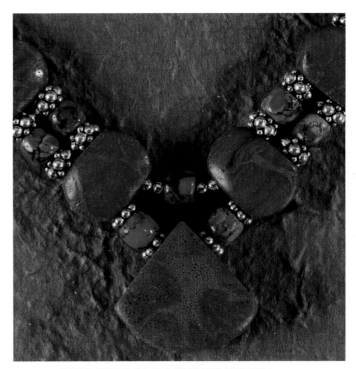

STEP 3: DETAIL OF THE PENDANT SECTION.

# FINISHING THE STRANDS

**1.** Repeat Pattern 2 (Figure 4-6) and thread on a coral bead.

**2.** Repeat Pattern 1 (Figure 4-4) twice more, being sure to thread on a coral bead after each repeat.

**3.** Repeat Pattern 2 (Figure 4-6) and thread on a coral bead.

**4.** Repeat Pattern 1 (Figure 4-4) twice more, being sure to thread on a coral bead after each repeat.

**5.** Repeat Pattern 2 (Figure 4-6) and thread on a coral bead.

**6.** Repeat Pattern 1 (Figure 4-4) once more. Pull wires up snugly, but not tight.

# ADDING THE CLASP

**1.** Take both wire ends through the other end of the clasp.

**2.** Tie wires together in an overhand knot.

**3.** Thread wire ends through a crimp bead and push it down against the knot.

**4.** Use crimp pliers to close and secure the crimp bead.

**5.** Trim wire ends close to crimp for the finished ends shown below.

STEP 5: FINISHED ENDS OF THE NECKLACE.

IF YOU ARE HAVING TROUBLE FINDING TWO-HOLE BEADS, LOOK IN THE COSTUME JEWELRY SECTION OF YOUR FAVORITE DEPARTMENT STORE. MANY BRACELETS ARE MADE WITH TWO-HOLE BEADS. ALSO, LOOK IN SHOPS THAT SELL VINTAGE BEADS, AS MANY OF THEM ARE MADE WITH TWO HOLES.

**tip**

## MATERIALS (FOR BOTH 7" PURPLE BRACELETS)

- 16 purple-and-silver 11mm square strand spacers

- 15 purple-and-silver 10mm x 14mm rectangular strand spacers

- 28 silver 4mm flat disc spacer beads

- 4 silver 3mm round beads

- Silver two-strand clasp

- 4 silver 2mm crimp beads

- 18" bright Beadalon® 49-strand .018"-diameter stringing wire

- Double wrist measurement plus • 6" Beadalon® .031"-diameter Elasticity™

- Scissors

- Wire cutters

- Crimp pliers

- Bead sorting dish or cloth

- Tape measure

## MATERIALS (FOR BOTH 7" BLUE BRACELETS)

- 16 blue-and-silver 9mm square strand spacers

- 16 clear-and-silver 10mm square strand spacers

- 30 silver 2.5mm round beads

- 4 silver 2mm crimp beads

- Silver two-strand clasp

- 18" bright Beadalon® 49-strand .018"-diameter stringing wire

- Double wrist measurement plus 6" Beadalon® .031"-diameter Elasticity™

- Same tools as above

## USING MULTIPLE-HOLE BEADS

# DECORATIVE SPACERS BRACELETS

These decorative strand spacers are normally used as accents in two-strand projects. Used alone or with a few beads, they make very striking projects. We've done similar bracelets on elastic and wire to give you more ideas to chose from.

## MAKING THE PURPLE ELASTIC BRACELET

1. Cut elastic in half so you have two pieces that are your wrist measurement plus 3".

2. Alternate threading onto one elastic piece one rectangular spacer with one square spacer until you have enough to go around your wrist. Be sure to end with the square spacer, but just pass through one hole.

3. Loosely knot elastic to hold beads in place.

4. Pass through the second set of holes in the spacer beads with the second piece of elastic. Just thread on one hole of the last square spacer.

5. Pass the beginning ends of elastic through the other hole in the last square spacer.

6. Tie each set of the ends of elastic into a surgeon's knot, as shown on page 18. Knots should be hidden inside back of square spacer.

7. Trim ends.

## MAKING THE BLUE ELASTIC BRACELET

Follow instructions for the purple elastic bracelet, but alternate the blue-and-silver and the clear-and-silver squares in place of the purple ones.

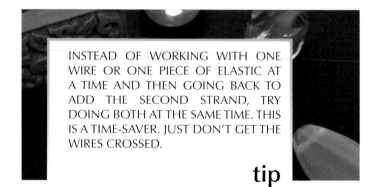

INSTEAD OF WORKING WITH ONE WIRE OR ONE PIECE OF ELASTIC AT A TIME AND THEN GOING BACK TO ADD THE SECOND STRAND, TRY DOING BOTH AT THE SAME TIME. THIS IS A TIME-SAVER. JUST DON'T GET THE WIRES CROSSED.

**tip**

# MAKING THE PURPLE WIRE BRACELET

1. Cut wire in half so you have two 9" pieces. Use more wire if needed on a larger wrist.

2. Thread one wire through a crimp bead, through one hole of one end of the clasp and pass wire end back through crimp, leaving a ½" tail.

3. Use crimp pliers to close and secure the crimp bead.

4. Repeat steps 2 and 3 for the other wire.

5. Thread one 3mm silver round bead onto one wire.

6. Thread onto the same wire one spacer bead, one square, one spacer and one rectangle bead. Repeat this pattern, as shown, until you have six rectangles.

7. End strand with one spacer, one square, one spacer and one 3mm silver round bead.

8. Thread on a crimp bead, pass wire end through other end of clasp, back through the crimp bead and through about ½" of the beaded strand. Pull snugly.

9. Use crimp pliers to close and secure the crimp bead.

10. Trim wire end close to the beads.

11. Repeat steps 5 through 10 for other wire strand for the finished look shown.

# MAKING THE BLUE WIRE BRACELET

1. Follow steps 1 through 5 from the purple wire bracelet instructions.

2. Alternately thread on one round bead, one blue square, one 3mm silver round bead and one clear square, as shown below, until you get the length desired.

3. End strand with one 3mm silver round bead.

4. Follow steps 8 through 11 from the purple wire bracelet instructions for the finished look shown below.

STEP 6: PATTERN REPEAT.

STEP 11: FINISHED ENDS OF THE PURPLE WIRE BRACELET.

STEP 2: PATTERN REPEAT.

STEP 4: FINISHED ENDS OF THE BLUE WIRE BRACELET.

## MATERIALS

- 3 red 24mm x 17mm carved cinnabar beads
- 6 Bali silver 4mm x 6mm beads
- 6 silver 2.5mm round beads
- 3 silver 2" head pins
- 1 pair silver earring findings
- Silver pendant bale
- 20" silver snake chain
- Round nose pliers
- Chain nose pliers
- Wire cutters
- Bead sorting dish or cloth

## USING HEAD/EYE PINS

# CINNABAR SET

Cinnabar is a heavy bright red mineral and is the principal ore of mercury. Some antique Chinese carved beads were made from this material before the harmful effects of mercury were known. These particular Chinese beads are carved from some type of resin.

# INSTRUCTIONS

**1.** Thread onto each head pin one 2.5mm silver round bead, one Bali silver bead, one cinnabar bead, one Bali silver bead and another 2.5mm silver round bead.

**2.** Trim head pin ends to ³/₈" and turn loops on all pins, referring to the instructions for turning loops on page 21 or wrapped loops on page 23, if needed.

**3.** Attach the pendant bale to one pin and hang it on the chain for the necklace.

**4.** Attach the remaining two pins to the earring findings.

WHEN ATTACHING JUMP RINGS OR PIN LOOPS TO EACH OTHER OR TO FINDINGS, AS IN STEPS 3 AND 4, BEND THE LOOP/JUMP RING SIDE-TO-SIDE TO OPEN (FIGURE 4-9, TOP VIEW OF JUMP RING). DO NOT SPREAD ENDS AWAY FROM EACH OTHER IN A DIRECT LINE.

INCORRECT          CORRECT

**tip**

## MATERIALS

- 6 clear aurora borealis 9mm x 6mm faceted crystals (A)
- 12 teal aurora borealis 6mm bicone crystals (B)
- 32 Bali silver 4mm daisy spacer beads (C)
- 4 Bali silver 3mm x 5mm spacer beads (D)
- 10 silver 3mm round beads (E)
- 2 Bali silver 2½" head pins
- 4 Bali silver 2" head pins
- 2 silver three-hole-to-one findings
- 10 silver 4mm jump rings
- 1 pair silver earring findings
- Round nose pliers
- Chain nose pliers
- Wire cutters
- Bead sorting dish or cloth

## USING HEAD/EYE PINS

## BEAD KEY

9mm x 6mm clear aurora borealis faceted crystals (A)

6mm teal aurora borealis bicone crystals (B)

ooo 4mm Bali silver daisy spacer beads (C)

OOO 3mm x 5mm Bali silver spacer beads (D)

O 3mm silver round beads (E)

# TEAL AND CRYSTAL EARRINGS

Swarovski crystals provide the glitter in this pair of contemporary earrings.

# INSTRUCTIONS

FIGURE 4-10

**1.** Refer to Bead Key on the facing page and thread beads onto one 2" head pin in the following sequence (Figure 4-10): C-B-C-A-C-B-C-E-C-E.

**2.** Turn the end of the pin into a wrapped loop, referring to the instructions for making wrapped loops on page 23, if needed.

**3.** Repeat steps 1 and 2 on the remaining three 2" head pins. Set all four pins aside.

**4.** Refer again to the Bead Key and thread beads onto each of the 2½" head pins in the following sequence (Figure 4-11): C-B-C-D-C-A-C-D-C-B-C-E.

FIGURE 4-11

**5.** Repeat step 2 for the other 2½" head pin.

**6.** Use jump rings to attach each 2½" beaded head pin to the center loop of each three-hole finding.

**7.** Use jump rings to attach each 2" beaded head pin to the outside loops of each three-hole finding.

**8.** Use jump rings to attach the top loop of each finding to each earring finding. (You may need two jump rings per finding to get the earrings to hang correctly.)

## MATERIALS

- 12 pink 10mm x 8mm twisted oval beads (A)
- 15 pink 9mm twisted round beads (B)
- 8 silver fire-polished 4mm faceted beads (C)
- 7mm silver twisted tube bead (D)
- 18 silver 4mm x 6mm flower beads (E)
- 15 silver 4mm flat flower spacer beads (F)
- 9 silver 2" head pins
- 1½" silver eye pin
- 16" silver ball chain necklace
- 1 pair silver earring findings
- Round nose pliers
- Chain nose pliers
- Wire cutters
- Bead sorting dish or cloth

## USING HEAD/EYE PINS

## BEAD KEY

10mm x 8mm pink twisted oval beads (A)

9mm pink twisted round beads (B)

4mm silver fire-polished faceted beads (C)

7mm silver twisted tube bead (D)

4mm x 6mm silver flower beads (E)

 4mm silver flat flower spacer beads (F)

# BALL CHAIN NECKLACE

Ball chain makes a nice necklace from which to hang head pins. The balls are evenly spaced, which makes it easy to place the head pins.

# CREATING THE DANGLES

**1.** Refer to the Bead Key and thread beads onto the eye pin in the following bead sequence (Figure 4-12): C-D-C.

**2.** Trim pin and make loop on open end, referring to the instructions for making a loop on page 21 or page 23 for a wrapped loop, if needed. Set pin aside.

**3.** Refer to the Bead Key again and thread beads onto one head pin in the following bead sequence (Figure 4-13): F-A-E-B-E-A-E.

**4.** Trim pin and make loop on open end, as in step 2 for the eye pin.

**5.** Repeat steps 3 and 4 twice more, making a total of three beaded head pins. These are #1 pins.

**6.** Refer to the Bead Key and thread beads onto one head pin in the following bead sequence (Figure 4-14): F-C-B-E-A-E-B-F.

**7.** Trim pin and make loop on open end, as in step 4.

**8.** Repeat steps 6 and 7 five more times, making a total of six beaded head pins. These are #2 pins.

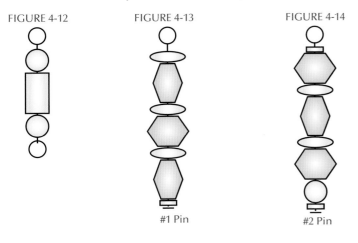

FIGURE 4-12     FIGURE 4-13     FIGURE 4-14

#1 Pin          #2 Pin

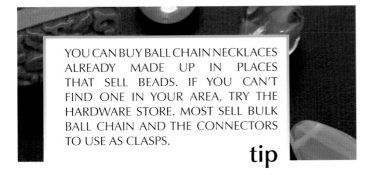

YOU CAN BUY BALL CHAIN NECKLACES ALREADY MADE UP IN PLACES THAT SELL BEADS. IF YOU CAN'T FIND ONE IN YOUR AREA, TRY THE HARDWARE STORE. MOST SELL BULK BALL CHAIN AND THE CONNECTORS TO USE AS CLASPS.

**tip**

# ATTACHING THE DANGLES TO NECKLACE

**1.** Count the balls on the ball chain. Be sure there is an even number. If not, remove one ball at the end of the chain, as shown, with wire cutters.

**2.** Carefully twist one loop of the eye pin open and attach it to a #1 pin.

**3.** Attach the other end of the eye pin between the center two balls of the necklace for the center dangle.

**4.** Move over two balls on one side of center and attach a #2 pin. Repeat on other side of necklace two balls over from center.

**5.** Move over two balls on both sides and attach a #1 pin.

**6.** Move over two more balls on either side and attach a #2 pin for the finished look shown below.

STEP 1: The connector on a ball chain allows the versatility of removing balls from the end without affecting your ability to still attach the connector for a clasp afterward.

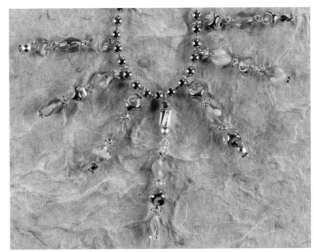

STEP 6: THE CENTER OF THE NECKLACE WITH ALL OF THE DANGLES ATTACHED.

# MAKING THE EARRINGS

**1.** Carefully twist the loop of a #2 pin and attach it to an earring finding.

**2.** Repeat with last #2 pin and other earring finding.

## USING MEMORY WIRE

### BEAD KEY

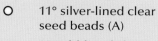

- ○ 11° silver-lined clear seed beads (A)
- ○ 6° gold-lined clear seed beads (B)
- ◇ 6mm clear bicone faceted beads (C)
- ⬤ Gold memory wire end caps (D)
- △ Brass charms (E)

# WINE GLASS TAGS

Wine glass tags are fun projects to make with memory wire. The ring wire is just the right size to fit around a wine glass stem. Use different charms or different colors of beads to keep the tags unique.

# BEADING THE RINGS

**1.** Break off a piece of memory wire approximately 3" long.

**2.** Glue a memory wire end cap onto one end (Figure 4-15). Be careful not to glue your fingers.

**3.** Refer to the Bead Key on the facing page and thread beads onto the wire in the following sequence (Figure 4-16): A-B-A-B-A-B-A-B-A-B-A-B-A-B-A-C-A-C-A-B-A-B-A-B-A-B-A-B-A-B-A.

**4.** Push the beads tightly against each other on wire and place a tiny drop of glue on the last A bead to hold all of the beads in place. Let glue set.

**5.** Break off wire about ⅛" beyond end of beads.

**6.** Glue the other end cap on the remaining wire end (Figure 4-17).

**7.** Repeat steps 1 through 6 three more times.

# MAKING THE DANGLE

**1.** Refer to the Bead Key and thread beads onto one eye pin in the following sequence (Figure 4-18): A-C-A.

**2.** Push beads tightly against the loop, bend the remainder of the pin in a right-angle with pliers (Figure 4-19) and trim end to ⅜".

**3.** Use round nose pliers to turn a loop in end of pin (Figure 4-20).

**4.** Thread on a brass charm in loop before closing it and then close the loop to attach the charm to the beaded eye pin dangle (Figure 4-21).

**5.** Attach the beaded eye pin dangle to the beaded ring by opening the top pin loop and bending it around the ring between the two center clear bicone (C) beads (Figure 4-22).

**6.** Repeat steps 1 through 5 with the three remaining pins and beaded loops for the four finished varieties shown.

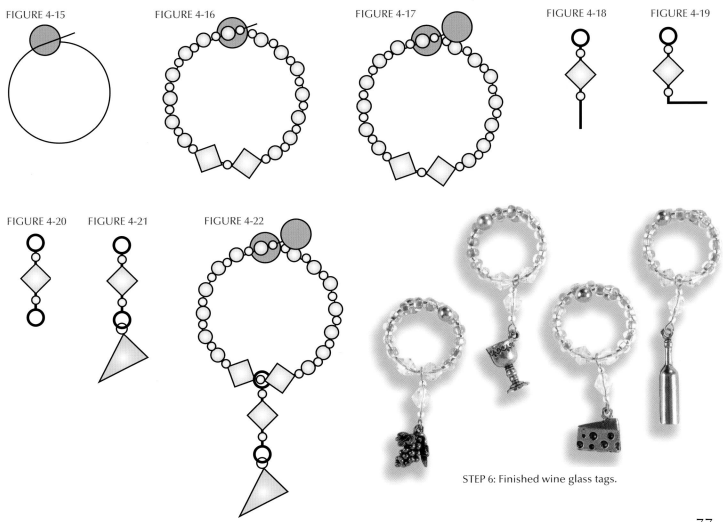

FIGURE 4-15   FIGURE 4-16   FIGURE 4-17   FIGURE 4-18   FIGURE 4-19

FIGURE 4-20   FIGURE 4-21   FIGURE 4-22

STEP 6: Finished wine glass tags.

## MATERIALS (FOR 7" RED-AND-SILVER BRACELET)

• 2 pieces (wrist measurement plus 1") bracelet memory wire

• 112 silver 2.5mm round beads

• 9 red crystal-and-silver 7mm x 11mm two-hole strand spacers

• 4 silver 3mm round memory wire end caps

• Super Glue

• Chain nose pliers

• Tape measure

• Bead sorting dish or cloth

## MATERIALS (FOR 7" BLACK FACETS BRACELET)

• 2 pieces (wrist measurement plus 1") memory wire

• 13 clear aurora borealis Swarovski crystal-and-silver 10mm x 15mm strand spacers

• 24 black Swarovski aurora borealis 6mm bicone crystals

• Same tools as above

## MATERIALS (FOR 7" TURQUOISE BRACELET)

• 2 pieces (wrist measurement plus 1") memory wire

• 4 silver pointed memory wire end caps

• 9 turquoise 8mm x 18mm two-hole beads

• 16 turquoise 7mm round beads

• 36 copper 4mm round beads

• 32 silver 4mm flat spacer beads

• Super Glue

• Same tools as above

## USING MEMORY WIRE

# TWO-STRAND MEMORY WIRE BRACELETS

You can use more than one strand of memory wire in a project as shown in these bracelets. The wires will need to be the same length to make the process work correctly. This is an excellent place to use the memory wire end caps, though a loop at the end would also work.

# RED-AND-SILVER BRACELET

This delicate bracelet is made using crystal-and-silver two-hole strand spacers and tiny round silver beads. For best results, be sure your memory wire is exactly the same length.

## INSTRUCTIONS

**1.** Break off two pieces of wire 1" longer than your wrist measurement.

**2.** Glue a memory wire end cap on one end of each piece of wire. Let dry.

**3.** Thread three of the 2.5mm silver round beads onto each piece of wire.

**4.** Pass each wire through one hole of a red crystal-and-silver strand spacer. Be sure the front of the spacer faces out from the curve of the wire.

**5.** Thread five 2.5mm silver round beads on each wire and one more strand spacer, again making sure the spacer faces out. Repeat this pattern, as shown at right, until you have nine spacers or the length you need. (If you need additional length to finish the pattern, you have an extra 1" to work with.)

**6.** Thread three round beads onto each wire.

**7.** Push all the beads up against the first end caps until they are snug and glue the last three beads in place on each wire by running a drop of glue down the end of the wire into the beads. Let dry.

**8.** Break off excess wire ¹/₁₆" away from beads.

**9.** Glue the last two end caps in place for the finished look shown at far right.

STEP 5: Beading pattern.

STEP 9: Round end caps finish this bracelet.

This bracelet provides an extra amount of flash for that special occasion because it has crystals in the two-hole spacers and between them.

## INSTRUCTIONS

**1.** Break off two pieces of wire 1" longer than your wrist measurement.

**2.** Use round nose pliers to turn a loop in one end of each piece of wire.

**3.** Pass each wire through one hole of a strand spacer, making sure the strand spacer faces out from the curve of the wire.

**4.** Thread a crystal onto each wire.

**5.** Repeat steps 3 and 4, as shown at right, until you have the correct length for your wrist measurement.

**6.** Turn loops in ends of wire, as shown at far right, to secure the beads.

STEP 5: Beading pattern.

STEP 6: Looped ends finish this bracelet.

# TURQUOISE BRACELET

Turquoise gemstone beads are combined with silver and copper metal beads to make this delightful bangle.

## INSTRUCTIONS

**1.** Break off two pieces of memory wire 1" longer than your wrist measurement.

**2.** Glue a memory wire end cap on one end of each piece of wire. Let dry.

**3.** Thread a copper bead onto each wire.

**4.** Pass each wire through one hole of a large turquoise bead.

**5.** Thread onto each wire one copper bead, one silver spacer, one round turquoise, one silver spacer and one copper bead. Pass each wire through one hole of a large turquoise bead. Be sure domed part of beads face out.

**6.** Repeat step 5, as shown at right, until you have nine large turquoise beads or the number you need for your wrist measurement.

**7.** End each strand with one copper bead on each wire.

**8.** Glue the copper bead in place. Let dry.

**9.** Measure depth of hole in end cap and break off wire ends to this measurement.

**10.** Glue end caps in place for the look shown below.

STEP 6: Beading pattern.

STEP 10: Cone-shaped end caps finish this bracelet.

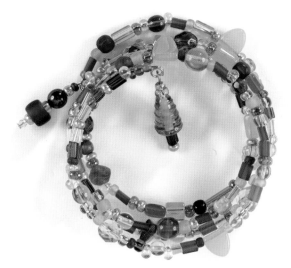

AN EVEN EASIER OPTION FOR USING MEMORY WIRE TO CREATE BRACELETS IS TO USE JUST ONE CONTINUOUS STRAND OF WIRE WITH BEADS THREADED ON, AS SHOWN AT LEFT. CREATE SUCH PIECES IN MUCH THE SAME WAY AS THE WINE GLASS TAGS, PAGES 76 AND 77, EXCEPT ATTACH THE DANGLES TO THE ENDS OF THE MEMORY WIRE, RATHER THAN TO THE CENTER.

## MATERIALS (FOR ONE ORNAMENT)

- 240 red or blue (or color of choice) 6° seed beads
- 30 bronze 6° seed beads
- 2 yards 28-gauge wire
- Monofilament line (optional)
- Chain nose pliers
- Needle nose pliers
- Bead sorting dish or cloth

## BEADS AND WIREWORK

# STAR ORNAMENTS

These ornaments are done with 6° seed beads on 28-gauge wire and measure about 4" across. You can make them with smaller beads, which will give you a nice size for a pendant or miniature ornament. Use a thinner wire with smaller beads. If you make them with larger beads, use a heavier wire.

# INSTRUCTIONS

1. Start with a piece of wire at least 2 yards long. Smooth it through your fingers a number of times to remove any kinks.

2. Thread on one bronze seed bead followed by two red/blue seed beads, until you have a total of 10 bronze and 20 colored beads.

3. Center the beads on the wire and pass one wire end through all the beads again. Pull up snugly, making a ring. You might want to twist the wires once to hold the beads in place at this point.

4. Pass each wire end through the next two red/blue beads and one bronze bead of the beaded circle (Figure 4-23).

5. Choose one wire end and thread on seven red/blue beads and one bronze bead (Figure 4-24).

6. Thread on three more red/blue beads, one bronze bead and three red/blue beads, and pass wire end back through the bronze bead from step 5 (Figure 4-25).

7. Thread on seven more red/blue beads and pass wire back through the second bronze bead over from where you exited the center ring (Figure 4-26).

8. Repeat steps 5 through 7 around the ring until you have five arms on the star (Figure 4-27).

9. Thread nine red/blue beads and one bronze bead onto the other wire end.

10. Thread on three more red/blue beads, one bronze bead and three red/blue beads, and pass wire end back through the bronze bead from step 9 (just as in step 6/ Figure 4-25).

11. Thread on nine red/blue beads and pass back into the center ring through the second bead over from where you exited with the second wire end (Figure 4-28).

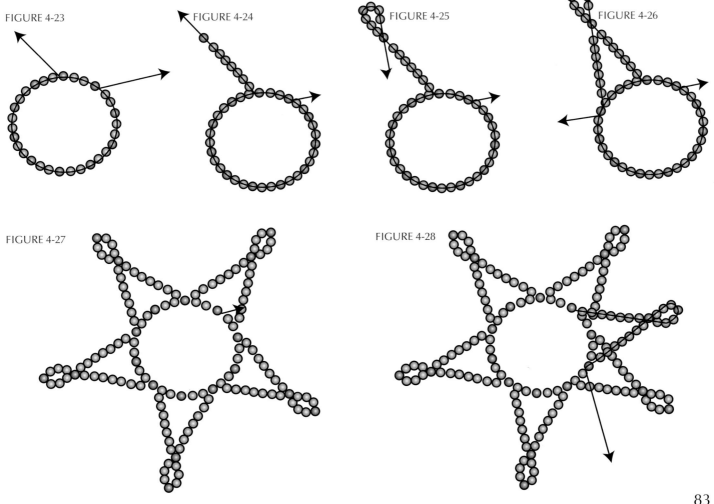

FIGURE 4-23

FIGURE 4-24

FIGURE 4-25

FIGURE 4-26

FIGURE 4-27

FIGURE 4-28

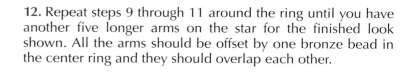

**12.** Repeat steps 9 through 11 around the ring until you have another five longer arms on the star for the finished look shown. All the arms should be offset by one bronze bead in the center ring and they should overlap each other.

**13.** Optional: Hang ornament from a piece of monofilament line or wire.

STEP 12: Finished ornament in two colors.

THE NECKLACE SHOWN AT THE RIGHT FIRST APPEARED IN *JEWELRY CRAFTS MAGAZINE*. IT IS MADE WITH ALEXANDRITE BEADS AND 32-GAUGE BRASS WIRE. DOUBLED WIRES ARE TWISTED TOGETHER FOR A SHORT LENGTH. A BEAD IS THREADED ON ONE WIRE AND THE WIRES ARE THEN TWISTED AGAIN, CAPTURING THE BEAD. THIS PROCESS IS REPEATED UNTIL THE LENGTH NEEDED IS ACHIEVED. NUMEROUS LENGTHS ARE THEN BRAIDED TOGETHER.

## MATERIALS

- Short-sleeved T-shirt
- 5 grams 11° seed beads (color darker than shirt)
- 350 to 400 pearl tiny teardrop beads
- 53 to 60 pearl 8° seed beads
- 3 yards sewing thread to match shirt
- #10 sharps needle
- Scissors
- Measuring tape
- Straight pins
- Bead sorting dish or cloth

## BEAD EMBROIDERY

# BEAD-EMBELLISHED SHIRT

An inexpensive T-shirt can be dressed up considerably by adding a few beads. You don't need to be an accomplished seamstress to do this project. You don't even need a pattern. Following the stitching on the shirt provides the only pattern necessary. Keep in mind that you need to plan a little stretch into your beadwork if the item of clothing goes on over the head.

# STITCHING THE NECKLINE

*Note:* The beading pattern does not go all around the neck and sleeves. You will need extra beads if you want to encircle all three.

**1.** Single-thread the needle with about 1 yard of thread. Tie a small knot in the very end and trim the thread tail.

**2.** Secure knot in seam on inside of neckband, starting 1" behind the shoulder seam, and bring needle out to front of band in the stitching line or against the edge of the neckband.

**3.** Thread on one of the 8° seed beads (Figure 4-29).

**4.** Pass needle back into the shirt to secure the bead (Figure 4-30).

**5.** Bring needle up again to the side of the bead in the direction you intend to go (Figure 4-31).

**6.** Thread on two seed beads, one teardrop and one seed bead. Then alternate teardrops and seed beads until you have seven teardrops. End stitch length with two seed beads (Figure 4-32).

**7.** Move over about ½" and pass back into the shirt (Figure 4-33). Note: The neckband stitching in the sample shirt is 10 stitches per 1", so I counted over five stitches and passed the needle back through the shirt.

**8.** Move over one stitch, bring needle back to the front of the shirt and thread on one 8° bead (Figure 4-34).

**9.** Pass back into the neckband where you just went down, looping the thread around the 8° bead (Figure 4-35) to secure it and to finish one pattern repeat (Figure 4-36).

**10.** Come up again next to the 8° bead and repeat step 6.

**11.** Repeat steps 7 through 9.

**12.** Continue in this manner, repeating steps 6 through 9, until you are 1" past the other shoulder seam. Finish beading with one 8° bead (Figure 4-37).

**13.** Bury and tie off thread in the seam line on the underside of the neckband for the finished look shown.

STEP 13: Finished stitching at the neckline.

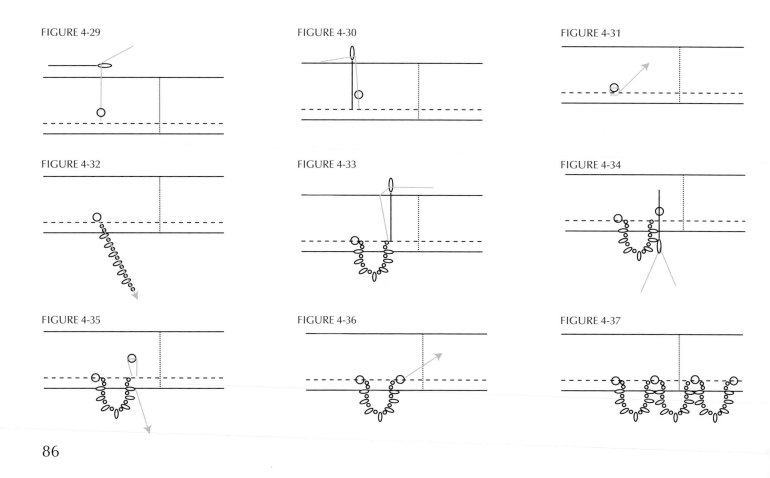

FIGURE 4-29

FIGURE 4-30

FIGURE 4-31

FIGURE 4-32

FIGURE 4-33

FIGURE 4-34

FIGURE 4-35

FIGURE 4-36

FIGURE 4-37

# STITCHING THE SLEEVES

**1.** Lay shirt flat and find the top center of the sleeve. Measure down on the front side about 3¾" and mark with a straight pin.

**2.** Repeat the steps 1 through 13 from Stitching the Neckband for about 7½" across the top of one sleeve. You can use the hemline as a guide for placement.

**3.** Repeat steps 1 and 2 for the other sleeve for the finished look shown below.

STEP 3: The finished shirt

- Lamp with six-section ecru shade
- 3"-long beaded fringe (enough to go around lampshade bottom plus 6")
- 20 grams silver-lined amber 11° seed beads
- FabriTac glue
- Nymo B thread
- #10 sharps needle
- Scissors
- Tracing paper
- Straight pins
- Pencil
- Disappearing marker
- Bead sorting dish or cloth

## BEAD EMBROIDERY

# BEADED LAMPSHADE

An inexpensive table lamp can be turned into a family heirloom by the addition of stitched beads and beaded fringe. Beaded fringe is readily available and relatively inexpensive to use. This project uses fringe, beads from the fringe and seed beads to create the pattern.

## GATHERING THE BEADS

**1.** Measure enough fringe to go around the inside of the bottom of the lampshade and cut a piece to that length.

**2.** Cut the beads from the remaining 6" of fringe.

**3.** Sort beads by size into the sorting dish and set aside.

## DRAWING THE PATTERN

**1.** Trace the full-size pattern (Figure 4-38) using tracing paper and a pencil. Use a copy machine to enlarge or reduce pattern to customize to the size of your lampshade, if desired.

**2.** Place tracing paper with design under the shade and pin in place with straight pins.

**3.** Turn on the lamp light.

**4.** Trace the pattern onto the shade with a disappearing marker (so the marks are not permanent).

**5.** Repeat steps 2 through 4 as many times as desired around the shade.

FIGURE 4-38

# STITCHING THE PATTERN

**1.** Single-thread the needle with about 1 yard of thread and tie a knot in the end of the thread.

**2.** Bring needle up from the inside of the shade at the bottom end of one of the spiral patterns.

**3.** Thread on four seed beads (Figure 4-39; figures show a side view).

**4.** Lay beads against the pattern marked on the shade and take needle back to the underside of the shade, tight against the end of the beads (Figure 4-40). Pull all thread through until snug but not tight.

**5.** Pass the needle back through the shade in the first hole, through all the beads again and thread on four more beads (Figure 4-41).

**6.** Pass the needle back into the shade, up through the second hole you made and back through the last four beads you picked up (Figure 4-42). You are backstitching the beads onto the pattern.

**7.** Thread on four more beads and continue backstitching until the end of the pattern. You may need fewer than four beads to finish out the pattern.

**8.** Pick out a bicone bead (which is what is used in the sample) from the fringe or a similar-sized round bead to use at the end of each spiral.

**9.** Bring needle up from the underside of the shade, thread on a bicone bead and one seed bead, pass back into the bicone and then to the underside of the shade (Figure 4-43). The seed bead will cover the hole in the bicone.

**10.** Repeat steps 1 through 9 for all patterns around the shade for the finished loop shown below.

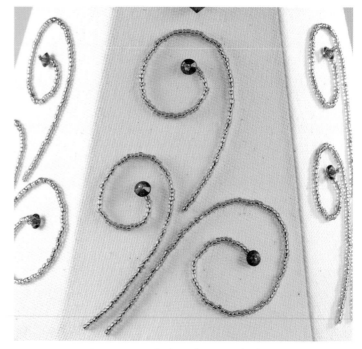

STEP 10: Detail of stitching on shade.

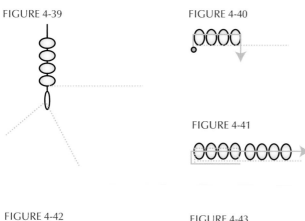

FIGURE 4-39

FIGURE 4-40

FIGURE 4-41

FIGURE 4-42

FIGURE 4-43

# MAKING TOP LOOPS

1. Single-thread the needle and tie a knot in the end of the thread.

2. Bring needle from the inside out to the front of the shade, close to the edge and on one of the seams.

3. Thread on a small round bead, pass back into the shade, around the rib of the shade and come out on the other side of the bead.

4. Thread on 10 seed beads, one bicone, five seed beads, one small round, one large teardrop, one small round, five seed beads, one bicone and 10 seed beads (Figure 4-44).

5. Pass needle to underside on the next seam, pass around the rib and come back to the front.

6. Repeat steps 2 through 5 around the top of the shade for the look shown below.

7. Tie off thread on the underside of the shade.

STEP 6: Detail of top dangle loops.

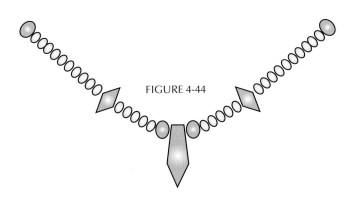

FIGURE 4-44

# ADDING THE FRINGE

1. Glue fringe to inside bottom edge of the shade, as shown below. Let dry.

2. Place shade on lamp.

STEP 1: Detail of the bottom fringe.

## MATERIALS

- 40mm x 30mm Mookite cabochon
- 40mm x 30mm gold cabochon setting
- 74 assorted Mookite beads*
- 38 brass 4mm flat spacer beads*
- 26 gold-plated 8° seed beads
- 4 gold-plated 11° seed beads
- Gold toggle clasp
- 3 gold 5mm split rings
- 2 gold 2mm crimp beads
- 30" bright Beadalon® 49-strand .018"-diameter stringing wire
- 20" gray 20# braided filament line
- Size 10 or 12 beading needle
- Gem glue
- Wire cutters
- Burnisher
- Jewelry pliers
- Split ring pliers
- Crimp pliers
- Bead sorting dish or cloth
- Beading board

*The number of beads needed are approximate, as your beadwork may require slightly more or less depending on the length of the strand.

## SIMPLE BEADED CABOCHON

# MOOKITE NECKLACE

One of my favorite things to do in beading is use a cabochon—a domed and polished gemstone—in a piece of jewelry. Cabochons are usually carved from semiprecious stones, but they can be made from all sorts of materials: shell, bone, plastic, polymer clay, metal or glass. I have even used antique buttons as cabochons. Because cabochon pieces usually require a more advanced set of skills, the ones shown in this piece are very simple with a manufactured cabochon setting as a base. Mookite is a semiprecious gemstone material that has a variety of colors in each piece. The colors range from off-white to mustard yellow to a milky burgundy. No two pieces will ever look alike. You can find a wide range of beads cut from Mookite. It has a nice polish and creates an attractive piece of jewelry.

## Embellishing the Finding

Because the purchased finding is rather plain, you might want to make it more attractive by adding gold beads around the outside. If you do not wish to embellish the finding, you can skip this optional section and go right to the Setting the Stone section.

**1.** Single-thread the needle with the braided filament line.

**2.** Pull needle through one hole of the finding from the inside, leaving a 4" tail of thread inside.

**3.** Thread on a gold 8° bead, pass needle back through same hole, hold both ends of the thread and pull snugly (Figure 4-45; side view of the finding).

**4.** Pass needle to the next hole and repeat step 3 (Figure 4-46).

**5.** Continue around the finding as in step 4, adding a bead in every hole (Figure 4-47).

**6.** Tie the ends of the threads together in an overhand knot when you get back to where you started and trim thread tails to ½".

## Setting the Stone

**1.** Insert one end of the 30" piece of stringing wire through the finding about one-quarter of the way down one side, pass wire across finding and out corresponding hole on other side (Figure 4-48). Center the finding on the wire length.

**2.** Put gem glue on the back of the cabochon to within ¼" of edge.

**3.** Place cabochon into the finding, being sure to catch ends of braided filament under the stone for the look shown. Allow glue to dry completely before proceeding with the next steps.

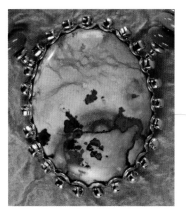

STEP 3: Once dry, the embellished cabochon is ready to become the centerpiece of the necklace.

FIGURE 4-45

FIGURE 4-46

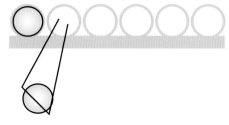

FIGURE 4-47

FIGURE 4-48

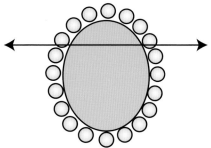

# MAKING THE NECKLACE

**1.** Use split ring pliers to attach one split ring to the loop end of the toggle clasp. Set aside.

**2.** Use split ring pliers to hook two split rings together and attach one to the bar end of the toggle clasp. Set aside.

**3.** Arrange the remaining beads in your own pattern on the bead board. Intermix sizes and shapes.

**4.** Thread onto one side of the necklace two 11° seed beads and then add the beads as you have laid them out (Figure 4-49).

FIGURE 4-49

**5.** Finish the strand with one 8° gold seed bead and a crimp bead when you are about ¾" from the end of the wire.

**6.** Pass wire end through a split ring on one half of the toggle clasp, back through the crimp bead and through about ½" of beads on the strand. Pull up wire snugly but not too tightly.

**7.** Use crimp pliers to close and secure the crimp bead.

**8.** Trim wire end close to the beading.

**9.** Repeat steps 4 through 8 for the other side of the necklace for the finished look shown below.

STEP 9: Finished ends of the necklace.

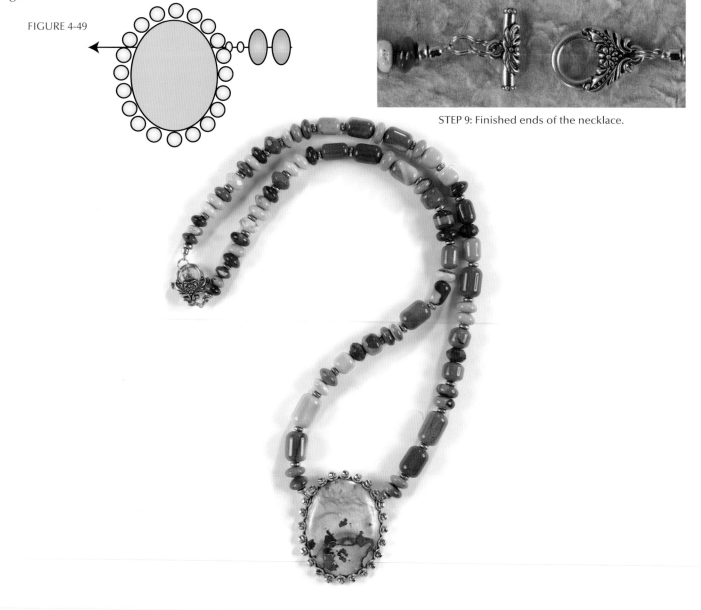

## MATERIALS

- 10 grams #DB103 raspberry-and-gold luster Delica beads
- 5 grams #DB310 black matte Delica beads
- 32 #DB022 bronze metallic Delica beads
- 32 bronze fire-polished 4mm round faceted beads
- 1" pin backing
- Black Silamide thread
- Size 12 beading needle
- 1⅝" x 1¼" piece black Ultrasuede®
- 1⅝" x 1¼" piece dark plastic or cardstock
- Loom
- Chalk pencil
- Scissors
- Bead sorting dish or cloth
- FabriTac glue
- Cellophane tape

## LOOM WEAVING

# LOOMED BROOCH

This brooch is made with Delica beads. Delicas are uniform cylindrical Japanese beads that are smaller than 11° seed beads. They are used for any kind of bead weaving that requires uniformity. They have color numbers so it is easy to duplicate any pattern done in Delicas. Fringe is another option for using the warp threads.

# WEAVING THE BROOCH

1. Follow the Threading a Loom steps from the Weaving a Bracelet instructions on page 25, except make the warp 32 threads wide. Because the Delicas are very small, run the threads between each coil of the spring.

2. Go up and back down the loom, being very careful not to cross the warp threads as you put them on the hook at either end. This will be very important later.

3. Start against one end and weave the pattern from the top down as in the Weaving a Bracelet instructions on page 26, being sure to follow the pattern for this piece (Figure 4-50).

4. Work the thread tails in after you complete the tightening of the woven section.

5. Cut the threads at the bottom of the loom against the hook but not at the top.

6. Carefully lift the threads off the hook at top.

FIGURE 4-50

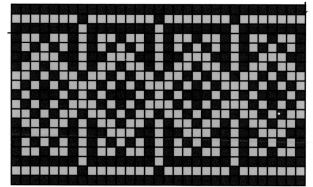

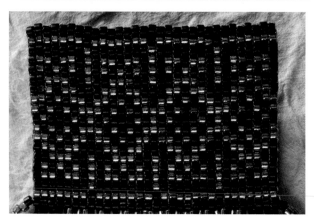

# TIGHTENING THE WOVEN SECTION

1. Place the woven piece on a hard, flat surface and tape the woven part of the design securely to this surface.

2. Lay warp threads out so they are like they were on the loom.

3. Place one hand on design to hold it securely.

4. Start at the side in which you started warping the loom and gently grasp the first two threads together at the ends.

5. Pull the threads towards the bottom until the threads are against the top of the woven piece.

6. Repeat steps 3 through 5 with the next two threads. Continue in the same manner across piece. If you haven't pierced a warp thread with the weft thread, this should work well. If you have, just pull the free thread.

7. Remove tape.

# ADDING THE FRINGE

1. Place a needle on an outside warp thread; either side of the piece is fine.

2. Thread on one black bead followed by five raspberry beads. Repeat this sequence four more times.

3. Thread on one faceted bronze bead and one bronze Delica (Figure 4-51).

4. Skip the last bronze Delica and pass the needle back through all the beads from steps 2 and 3. Pull up snugly so fringe lays against the base of the work with no thread showing.

5. Work the thread into the woven piece, tie a couple of half-hitch knots, glue the last knot and trim off the excess thread.

6. Repeat steps 1 through 5 for the next warp thread, except this time start with two black beads at the top of the fringe strand.

7. Continue adding one additional black bead at the top of each fringe strand until you get to five black beads (Figure 4-52).

8. Thread on one raspberry bead as you start the sixth fringe strand (Figure 4-53).

9. Continue adding one raspberry bead at the top of each fringe strand until you get to 11 raspberry beads. This should be the center of the piece.

10. Repeat steps 1 through 9 in reverse order to create the second half of the fringe for the finished look shown at top right on the next page. Because you have 32 threads, you will have two fringe strands with 11 raspberry beads at the top.

FIGURE 4-51:
The first fringe.

FIGURE 4-52:
The fifth fringe.

FIGURE 4-53:
The sixth fringe.

STEP 10: Detail of the finished fringe.

# FINISHING THE BROOCH

**1.** Cut a piece of plastic or cardstock slightly smaller than the woven area of the brooch.

**2.** Glue the plastic/cardstock to the back of the weaving.

**3.** Cut a piece of Ultrasuede the same size as the woven part of the brooch.

**4.** Center the pin backing on the upper half of the inside of the Ultrasuede piece.

**5.** Mark the ends of the pin with a chalk pencil.

**6.** Make a small slit at marks.

**7.** Place pin backing through slits so the backing is on inside and pin is on outside. Glue in place.

**8.** Glue Ultrasuede to back of woven part of pin for the finished back, as shown below.

STEP 8: The back of the brooch.

## MATERIALS (FOR LAVENDER BRACELET)

- 180 lavender 8° seed beads
- 70 yellow 8° seed beads
- 45 turquoise 8° seed beads
- Silamide thread in color to match the beads
- Gold two-strand box clasp
- 4 gold clamshell bead tips
- 4 gold 5mm split rings
  4 gold 2mm crimp beads
- Size 10 or 12 beading needle
- Loom
- Split ring pliers
- Round nose pliers
- Scissors
- Bead sorting dish or cloth
- Glue

## MATERIALS (FOR PINK-AND-BLUE BRACELET)

- 3 grams matte blue aurora borealis 11° seed beads
- 2 grams matte pink 11° seed beads
- Brown Silamide thread
- Round silver two-hole box clasp
- 4 silver clamshell bead tips
- 4 silver 2mm crimp beads
- Size 10 or 12 beading needle
- Same tools as above

## MATERIALS (FOR DESIGNER MIX BRACELET)

- 5 grams designer mix 11° seed beads
- Silamide thread in color to match the beads
- Gold two-strand box clasp
- 4 gold clamshell bead tips
- 4 gold 5mm split rings
- 4 gold 2mm crimp beads
- Size 10 or 12 beading needle
- Same tools as above

# LOOMED BRACELETS

One of the easiest projects to do on a loom is a simple band. The ones shown here have been turned into bracelets, but if you make them longer, they can be used as necklaces, hatbands or even belts. You can make your bands as wide as you want. Just be sure to add one string more than you have beads.

This bracelet uses 8° seed beads in a pattern of diamonds and crosses. It works up quickly in the larger beads. If you want to use smaller beads, you will need to make the bracelet longer.

## WEAVING THE BRACELET

1. Follow all steps for Weaving a Bracelet in the Weaving on a Loom section on pages 25 and 26, being sure to follow the pattern for this piece (Figure 4-54).

FIGURE 4-54

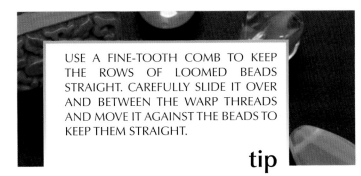

USE A FINE-TOOTH COMB TO KEEP THE ROWS OF LOOMED BEADS STRAIGHT. CAREFULLY SLIDE IT OVER AND BETWEEN THE WARP THREADS AND MOVE IT AGAINST THE BEADS TO KEEP THEM STRAIGHT.

**tip**

## FINISHING THE BRACELET

1. Thread one lavender bead onto each pair of threads (Figure 4-55). Thread a needle with these thread pairs if that is easier for you.

2. Place four threads together and pass through another lavender bead on each set of four (Figure 4-56).

3. Pass one set of four threads through the underside of a clamshell bead tip (Figure 4-57).

4. Split threads into groups of two (Figure 4-58).

5. Thread a crimp bead onto one set (Figure 4-58), tie off the threads against the crimp bead, glue the knot and trim the thread ends.

6. Close clamshell around knot (Figure 4-59).

7. Repeat steps 2 through 6 for the other set of four threads.

8. Work all thread tails into the piece, tying a few half-hitch knots as you go and trim the excess thread.

9. Repeat steps 1 through 8 on the other end of the bracelet.

10. Use split ring pliers to attach one split ring to each end of the clasp.

11. Attach clasp by bending the bars of the clamshell bead tips on each bracelet end around split rings in each end of the clasp.

FIGURE 4-55    FIGURE 4-56    FIGURE 4-57    FIGURE 4-58    FIGURE 4-59

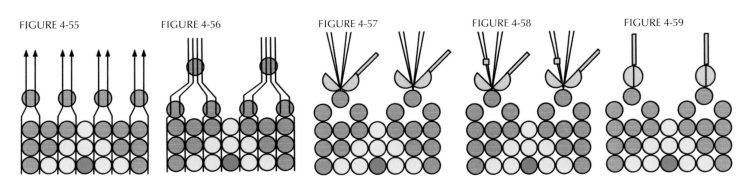

This bracelet is seven beads wide as well. Follow the instructions for the Lavender Loomed Bracelet, but substitute the pattern and materials for this piece.

## WEAVING THE BRACELET

**1.** Follow all steps for Weaving a Bracelet in the Weaving on a Loom section on pages 25 and 26, being sure to follow the pattern for this piece (Figure 4-60).

## FINISHING THE BRACELET

*Note*: Refer back to Figures 4-55 through 4-59 in the Lavender Loomed Bracelet instructions, page 99, for illustrated assistance, if necessary.

**1.** Thread two blue beads onto each pair of threads. Thread a needle with these thread pairs if that is easier for you.

**2.** Place four threads together and pass through another blue bead on each set of four.

**3.** Repeat steps 3 through 10 from the Lavender Loomed Bracelet instructions.

**4.** Attach clasp, as shown, by bending the bars of the clamshell bead tips on each bracelet end around split rings in each end of the clasp.

STEP 4: Clasp attached to each bracelet end.

FIGURE 4-60

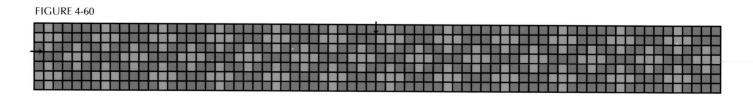

# DESIGNER MIX LOOMED BRACELET

This bracelet is the easiest of the three because there is no set pattern. The beads are from a designer bead mix. All you do is string them on just as you pick them up. You can make your own bead mix by putting four or five colors of seed beads together. Use 1 gram of each as you only need 4 to 5 grams to make this bracelet. This bracelet is also seven beads wide.

## WEAVING THE BRACELET

1. Follow all steps for Weaving a Bracelet in the Weaving on a Loom section on pages 25 and 26. There is no set pattern for this piece, so string beads on as you pick them up.

## FINISHING THE BRACELET

*Note:* Refer back to Figures 4-55 through 4-59 in the Lavender Loomed Bracelet instructions, page 99, for illustrated assistance, if necessary.

1. Thread two beads onto each pair of threads. Thread a needle with these thread pairs if that is easier for you.

2. Place four threads together and pass through another bead on each set of four.

3. Repeat steps 3 through 10 from the Lavender Loomed Bracelet instructions.

4. Attach clasp, as shown, by bending the bars of the clamshell bead tips on each bracelet end around split rings in each end of the clasp.

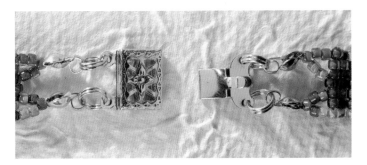

STEP 4: Clasp attached to each bracelet end. The clasp of the lavender bracelet would be similar to this one.

## MATERIALS (FOR 22" NECKLACE)

- 20mm round lavender art glass bead
- 2 lavender 13mm round art glass beads
- 36 silver 7mm x 5mm oval beads
- 14 lavender aurora borealis 6mm bicone crystals
- 6 silver 4mm round beads
- 8 grams lavender aurora borealis 11° seed beads
- Silver toggle clasp
- 2 silver clamshell bead tips
- 3 silver 5mm split rings
- 2 silver 2mm crimp beads
- 60" black Beadalon® DandyLine™ .008"-diameter thread
- Size 10 or 12 beading needle
- Scissors
- Gem glue
- Split ring pliers
- Round nose pliers
- Bead sorting dish or cloth

**WOVEN CHAINS**

# ART GLASS DAISY CHAIN NECKLACE

The inspiration for this necklace was the three focal beads. They are lampworked glass made by Denise Gaffey. The beads are an unusual color mix of milky purple, magenta and yellow. My original thought was to make them into a pendant, but this necklace is what happened instead. As you can see, the daisy chain can be dressed up significantly depending on the beads you use.

# BEGINNING THE NECKLACE

**1.** Single-thread the needle with about 36" of thread.

**2.** Tie one crimp bead on the very end of the thread, glue the knot and trim the thread end.

**3.** Thread on one clamshell bead tip from the inside, pass thread through until the crimp lays in the bowl of the clamshell and close clamshell around the crimp.

**4.** Thread on 16 seed beads and pass needle back through the first one you picked up (Figure 4-61).

**5.** Thread on a silver oval bead. Fit silver bead into the seed bead circle, so seed beads surround it. (You may need to adjust for size here. Add or subtract beads by even numbers only.)

**6.** Pass needle through the lower right bead—the ninth bead added when making the ring (Figure 4-62).

**7.** Thread on 14 seed beads and pass needle through the lower left bead of the previous pattern (Figure 4-63). This pattern is slightly different than other daisy chains. There should only be two seed beads between each oval bead here.

**8.** Thread on an oval bead and pass through the lower right bead of the pattern (Figure 4-63).

**9.** Repeat steps 7 and 8 once more. You should have three patterns with oval beads surrounded by seed beads.

**10.** Thread on 12 seed beads and pass needle through the lower left bead of the previous pattern (Figure 4-64).

**11.** Thread on a bicone crystal and pass through the lower right bead of this—the fourth—pattern (Figure 4-64).

**12.** Repeat steps 4 through 11 (the first four patterns), as shown, five more times for a total of 24 patterns.

FIGURE 4-61

FIGURE 4-62

FIGURE 4-63

FIGURE 4-64

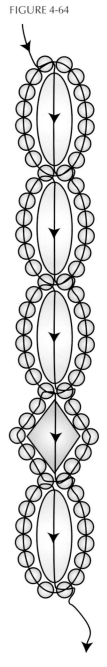

STEP 12: Detail of daisy chain pattern.

# ADDING THE ART GLASS BEADS

**1.** Thread on one 4mm round silver bead, one 13mm bead and one 4mm round.

**2.** Thread on 14 seed beads and pass back through the first seed bead picked up.

**3.** Thread on one crystal and pass through the lower left bead of the bicone pattern (Figure 4-64).

**4.** Thread on one 4mm round silver bead, the large art glass bead and one 4mm round.

**5.** Repeat steps 2 and 3.

**6.** Thread on one 4mm round silver bead, one 13mm bead and another 4mm round for the look shown below. Be sure to keep thread as tight as possible as you add the big beads.

STEP 6: Detail of art glass beaded section.

# MAKING THE OTHER NECKLACE HALF

The second half of the necklace is done in reverse order to the first half (steps 4 through 11 of Beginning the Necklace instructions).

**1.** Start with a crystal pattern by threading on 14 seed beads and passing back through the first seed bead picked up.

**2.** Thread on one crystal and pass through the lower left bead of the bicone pattern (Figure 4-64).

**3.** Make three silver oval patterns, as in steps 4 through 9 in Beginning the Necklace section.

**4.** Continue doing one crystal and three oval bead patterns until you have a total of 24 patterns.

# FINISHING THE NECKLACE

**1.** Thread on a clamshell from bottom up. Thread on a crimp bead.

**2.** Knot thread and tie off against crimp bead.

**3.** Close clamshell.

**4.** Attach one split ring to the loop end of the toggle.

**5.** Attach two split rings to the bar end of toggle.

**6.** Bend bars of clamshells around split rings for the finished ends shown below.

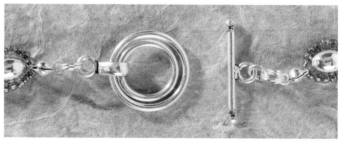

STEP 6: Finished ends with clasp.

## MATERIALS

- Cat accent bead
- 300 white 6° seed beads
- 200 black 6° seed beads
- 200 red 11° seed beads
- 14mm round silver two-strand box clasp
- 4 silver clamshell bead tips
- 4 silver 5mm split rings
- 4 silver 2mm crimp beads
- 144" black Beadalon® DandyLine™ .008"-diameter thread
- 2 size 10 beading needles
- Round nose pliers
- Split ring pliers
- Scissors
- Bead sorting dish or cloth

# LADDER STITCH CAT COLLAR

The black-and-white cat in this bead by Sharon Peters inspired this project. Black and white seemed the obvious choices for a color scheme. The red seed beads highlight and complement his nose and provide a needed spark of color.

*Note:* The instructions are given for the two-needle method. You can make this project with the one-needle method if you prefer.

# BEGINNING THE COLLAR

**1.** Cut two pieces of thread at least 30" long; use more if you can handle it.

**2.** Single-thread each needle and pull the threads through so they are the same length.

**3.** Tie a crimp bead on the end of each thread, glue the knots and trim thread tails.

**4.** Pass one needle through a clamshell bead tip from the inside and close the clamshell around the knot. Repeat with the other needle.

**5.** Attach split rings to one half of the clasp.

**6.** Bend the bar of one clamshell bead tip around one split ring. Repeat with the other clamshell bead tip.

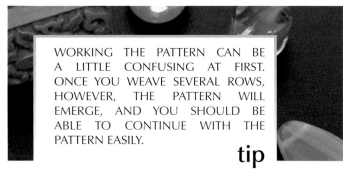

WORKING THE PATTERN CAN BE A LITTLE CONFUSING AT FIRST. ONCE YOU WEAVE SEVERAL ROWS, HOWEVER, THE PATTERN WILL EMERGE, AND YOU SHOULD BE ABLE TO CONTINUE WITH THE PATTERN EASILY.

**tip**

# WEAVING THE COLLAR

**1.** Refer to the pattern for the collar (Figure 4-65) and thread onto one needle one red bead and the beads from the first row of the pattern.

**2.** Thread one red bead on the second needle and pass through the beads on the first needle from the opposite direction. Refer to the basic instructions for double-needle ladder stitch, page 30, if needed.

**3.** Thread one red bead onto each needle.

**4.** Thread onto one needle the beads from the second row of the pattern, being sure you pick them up in the correct order for the previous row.

**5.** Continue picking up a red bead on each needle before you thread on the black and white beads and weave the pattern until you have half the length you need. *Note*: It makes a nicer looking collar if the center falls in the center of a pattern on the weaving.

**6.** Pull the beads up snugly.

FIGURE 4-65

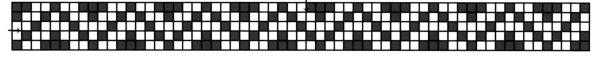

# ADDING THE CAT BEAD

**1.** Determine the top and bottom of the band when you get to the center of the collar.

**2.** Thread one red bead on the top needle (the one that comes out of the top of the band).

**3.** Thread three red beads and the cat bead on the bottom needle.

**4.** Thread the next row of black and white seed beads onto the second needle.

**5.** Pass the first (top) needle through the black and white seed beads (Figure 4-66).

**6.** Pass the top needle back through the red bead and the black-and-white row created before you added the cat bead.

**7.** Pass the bottom needle back through the three red beads, the cat bead and the black-and-white row created before you added the cat beads (Figure 4-67).

STEP 9: Reinforce the center where the heavy cat bead hangs.

**8.** Pass the top needle back through the red bead and the new black-and-white row.

**9.** Pass the bottom needle back through the three red beads, the cat bead and the new black-and-white row (Figure 4-68). You will pass through the center beads a total of three times to reinforce the center where the bead hangs, as shown at left.

# FINISHING THE NECKLACE

**1.** Add a red bead on each needle and continue following the pattern to weave the second half of the necklace.

**2.** Thread a red bead onto each needle when weaving is complete.

**3.** Thread a clamshell bead tip onto each needle from the bottom up.

**4.** Thread a crimp bead onto one needle, tie off the thread against the crimp bead, glue knot and trim thread end.

**5.** Close clamshell bead tip around knot.

**6.** Repeat steps 3 through 5 with the other needle.

**7.** Attach split rings to other half of clasp.

**8.** Bend bars of clamshells around split rings with round nose pliers for look of finished ends shown below.

STEP 8: Finished ends of collar with clasp.

WHEN CONTINUING ON AFTER STEP 4 OF FINISHING THE NECKLACE, IT IS A GOOD IDEA TO WEAVE THE BLACK-AND-WHITE PATTERN IN REVERSE ORDER FOR THE SECOND HALF OF THE NECKLACE, AS SHOWN IN THE MAIN PROJECT PHOTO ON PAGE 105.

**tip**

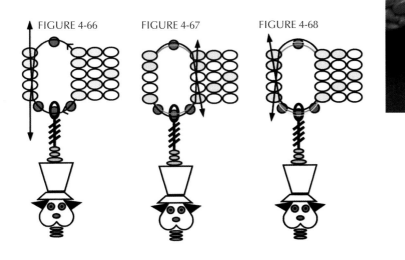

FIGURE 4-66          FIGURE 4-67          FIGURE 4-68

## MATERIALS (FOR 16" NECKLACE AND ONE PAIR EARRINGS)

- 14mm x 24mm turquoise slider bead
- 2 turquoise oval 12mm x 19mm beads
- 250 turquoise 4mm round beads
- 500 dark turquoise 8° seed beads
- 225 light turquoise 8° seed beads
- 2 silver 4mm round fluted beads
- 6 silver 4mm flat daisy spacer beads
- Silver toggle clasp
- 2 silver clamshell bead tips
- 2 silver 2mm crimp beads
- 3 silver 5mm split rings
- 2 silver 2" head pins
- 1 pair silver earring findings
- 1 spool black Beadalon® DandyLine™ .008"-diameter thread
- Size 10 beading needle
- Scissors
- Split ring pliers
- Round nose pliers
- Bead sorting dish or cloth

# SPIRAL ROPE JEWELRY SET

The color turquoise has long been a favorite of mine. When I saw this bead set by Bindy Lambell, I just had to have it. The large slider bead was the perfect fit for a spiral rope necklace. The round beads that came with the set were naturals for earrings. My bead stash had lots of colors of turquoise beads. Choose your favorite colors and see what you can weave.

# WEAVING THE NECKLACE

**1.** Cut as much thread as you can handle and single-thread the needle.

**2.** Weave a spiral rope, as in the basic instructions on page 31, designating the light turquoise seed beads for the core beads.

**3.** For the outside beads, thread on one dark turquoise seed bead, one 4mm round bead and another dark turquoise seed bead.

**4.** Continue weaving until desired length.

# FINISHING THE NECKLACE

**1.** Thread a daisy spacer and a 4mm round fluted bead onto one end of necklace.

**2.** Pass the needle through a clamshell bead tip from the underside.

**3.** Thread on a crimp bead, tie off the thread against the crimp bead, glue the knot and trim thread tail.

**4.** Close the clamshell around the crimp bead.

**5.** Repeat steps 1 through 4 on the other end of necklace for the finished look shown below.

**6.** Slide the slider bead onto the woven chain, as shown.

# MAKING THE EARRINGS

**1.** Thread one daisy spacer, one 4mm turquoise round bead, one 12mm x 19mm oval bead, one 4mm turquoise round bead and one daisy spacer onto one head pin.

**2.** Make a wrapped loop in the top of the pin, referring to the instructions on page 23, if needed.

**3.** Attach a split ring to the head pin and then to the earring finding.

**4.** Repeat steps 1 through 3 for the other earring.

STEP 5: Finished ends with clasp.

STEP 6: Position slider bead in the center of the woven chain.

## MATERIALS (FOR 25" NECKLACE)

- Shell pendant
- 250 white pearl 6° seed beads
- 250 white pearl 8° seed beads
- 500 gold-plated 11° seed beads
- 2,250 white pearl 14° seed beads
- 14mm gold round box clasp
- 2 gold clamshell bead tips
- 2 gold 2mm crimp beads
- White Nymo D thread
- Size 10 or 12 beading needle
- Scissors
- Gem glue
- Bead sorting dish or cloth

# DUTCH SPIRAL SHELL NECKLACE

This shell pendant has been in my possession for many years. It was purchased at a lighthouse gift shop on the Oregon coast. For many years, I wore it on a fiber necklace, but when I saw Cheryl Erickson's lacy spiral, I immediately made the necklace you see here.

# WEAVING THE NECKLACE

**1.** Cut as much Nymo thread as you can handle, single-thread the needle and pull on the thread to remove the stretch.

**2.** Follow the basic lacy spiral instructions on page 32, but add a gold 11° bead after the last 14° bead in each row. This will keep the 14° beads from slipping through the 6° beads and add a bit more color.

**3.** The second exception is to weave up to nine 14° beads, instead of seven as in the basic instructions.

**4.** Weave 23¾" and then start decreasing by one 14° bead in each row until you get to one.

# FINISHING THE NECKLACE

**1.** Thread a clamshell bead tip on one end from the bottom up.

**2.** Thread on a crimp bead, tie off thread against the crimp bead, glue the knot and trim the thread end.

**3.** Close the clamshell around the crimp.

**4.** Repeat steps 1 through 3 for other end of necklace.

**5.** Bend the bars of the clamshell bead tips around the loops in end of the clasp for the finished look shown.

**6.** Slide the shell pendant onto necklace, as shown.

STEP 5: The finished ends with clasp.

STEP 6: Front and back of the shell pendant after it is placed on the woven necklace.

111

## MATERIALS (FOR 7" BRACELET)

- 72 purple 4mm cube beads
- 48 bronze 4mm round beads
- 23 purple fire-polished 6mm crystals
- 46 purple 11° seed beads
- Gold toggle clasp
- 2 gold clamshell bead tips
- 3 gold split rings
- 2 gold 2mm crimp beads
- Size 10 beading needle
- 60" gray 20# Fireline™ fishing line
- Jewelry pliers
- Split ring pliers
- Jewelry glue
- Bead sorting dish or cloth
- Measuring tape
- Pencil and scrap paper

# EMBELLISHED POTAWATOMI BRACELET

The addition of crystals for embellishment on the basic Potawatomi weave makes this a very rich looking bracelet suitable for a night out on the town. Make up several in different color combinations. Don't be surprised if you get requests for this bracelet from your friends. The bracelet in the sample is several shades of purple. Since it may be difficult to find the exact colors I used, you may choose whatever colors appeal to you.

# MAKING THE BASIC BRACELET

1. Single-thread the needle with the entire length of fishing line.

2. Measure your wrist, subtract 1" and write down that number.

3. Follow the basic Potawatomi instructions on page 33, substituting the bronze 4mm round beads for the orange ones used in the basic example and the purple cube beads for the blue beads, and weave the length written down in step 2. *Note*: The way the beads lay against each other as you pull the thread snug makes the cube beads look like they are laying at angles to the round beads.

4. Finish this part of the bracelet by threading on one cube bead and one round bead and passing through the round bead from the last pass. These two beads should finish off the pattern.

5. Pass the thread back around the circle of beads and bring the needle out between the last two round beads.

6. Remove the needle and let the thread hang loose.

# EMBELLISHING THE BRACELET

1. Single-thread the needle with 1 yard of fishing line.

2. Pass needle between the two end round beads, leaving an 8" thread tail, and continue through one round bead, the cube bead and through the next two round beads (Figure 4-69).

3. Thread on one seed bead, one crystal and another seed bead (Figure 4-69).

4. Pass back into a round bead from the opposite side of the bracelet and through the second round bead (Figure 4-69). Pull beads snugly.

5. Pass through the cube bead and the two round beads of the next pattern (Figure 4-70).

6. Thread on one seed bead, one crystal and another seed bead (Figure 4-70).

7. Pass back through the round beads (Figure 4-70). You are actually making a loop around the round beads.

8. Continue pattern repeats across the bracelet in the same manner. You should have a crystal sitting atop every two round beads, except for either end of the bracelet.

9. Work the thread around until it comes out between the two round beads on the other end.

FIGURE 4-69

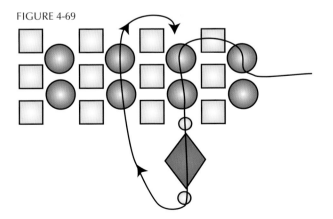

FIGURE 4-70

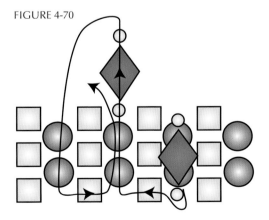

FIGURE 4-71

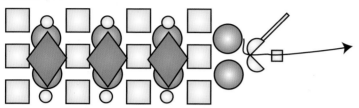

# FINISHING THE BRACELET

**1.** Thread a clamshell bead tip from the bottom up onto the thread tails on one end.

**2.** Thread on a crimp bead, pass one thread through the crimp bead and pull snugly (Figure 4-71). You want the clamshell to sit against the beading.

**3.** Tie off the threads against the crimp bead, glue the knot, trim the thread ends and close the clamshell.

**4.** Repeat steps 1 through 3 on the other end of the bracelet.

**5.** Bend the clamshell bar over the split ring.

**6.** Use split ring pliers to attach two split rings together and then attach one ring to the bar end of the toggle clasp and the other split ring to the clamshell as in the previous step for the finished look shown at left.

STEP 6: Finished ends with clasp.

## MATERIALS (FOR THE SET)

- 48 multicolored topaz 8mm round faceted beads (A)
- 54 bronze 4mm round beads (B)
- 42 bronze 6mm bicone beads (C)
- 90 bronze 11° seed beads (D)
- Yellow jade pendant
- 2 gold toggle clasps
- 12 gold jump rings
- 1 pair gold ball-and-loop earring findings
- 6 gold clamshell bead tips
- 6 gold 2mm crimp beads
- 88" Beadalon® 49-strand stringing wire
- Jewelry pliers
- Side cutters
- Bead sorting dish or cloth
- Tape measure

## BEAD KEY

 8mm round faceted multicolored topaz beads (A)

4mm round bronze beads (B)

6mm bronze bicone beads (C)

11° bronze seed beads (D)

## WEAVING STITCHES

# RIGHT-ANGLE WEAVE YELLOW JADE JEWELRY SET

I found this jade pendant at one of the gem shows in Tucson. It perfectly matched some glass beads I had purchased earlier that day. This set combines stringing with a basic right-angle weave. It is an easy, yet attractive, project.

# BEGINNING THE NECKLACE

1. Use the side cutters to cut two pieces of stringing wire each 24" long.  Set one wire piece aside.

2. Thread onto the other wire enough 11° bronze seed beads to equal the thickness of the jade pendant piece, pass the wire through the hole in the pendant, and center the beads and pendant in the middle of the wire.

3. Thread onto one end of the same wire one 4mm bronze round bead and enough bronze seed beads to clear the top of pendant. Pull beads up snugly. Repeat on the other end of the same wire.

FIGURE 4-72

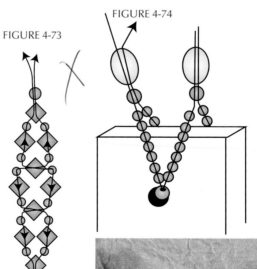

4. Place the ends of wire together and pass both through one 4mm bronze round bead followed by one 8mm topaz bead (Figure 4-72). Repeat this B-A pattern four more times.

# WEAVING THE PATTERN

1. Thread on one 4mm bronze round bead and a 6mm bronze bicone.

2. Split the wires and thread onto one wire a D-C-D pattern and a D-C-D-C pattern on the other wire (Figure 4-73).

FIGURE 4-73

3. Pass the first wire through the last C bead on the second wire from the opposite direction (Figure 4-73) and pull snugly.

4. Repeat steps 2 and 3.

5. Thread onto each wire a D-C-D pattern, place the wire ends together and pass both through a 6mm bronze bicone (Figure 4-73) for the look shown below.

STEP 5: The right-angle weave pattern.

# FINISHING THE NECKLACE

1. Continue to hold both wire ends together and thread on beads in the following sequence: B-A-B-A-B-A-B-A-B-A-B-A-B-A-B-A-B-A-B-A-B-A-B-A-B.

2. Pass both ends of wire through the bottom of a clamshell bead tip.

3. Thread a crimp bead onto one wire, tie off wires against the crimp bead and trim wires close to the knot.

4. Close the clamshell with pliers.

5. Take second 24" necklace wire through the B and D beads in the hole of the pendant (Figure 4-74).

6. Repeat steps 3 and 4 from the Beginning the Necklace section to attach the pendant, as shown below right.

7. Complete all steps in the Weaving the Pattern section and steps 1 through 4 in this Finishing the Necklace section to complete the second necklace strand.

8. Attach jump rings to both pieces of the toggle clasp as needed for length.

9. Bend each bar of the clamshell bead tips over the last jump ring attached to each end of the clasp for the finished look shown below.

FIGURE 4-74

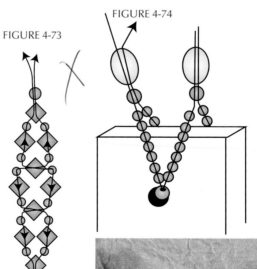

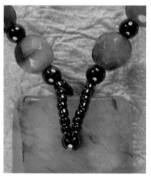

STEP 6: The pendant is attached.

STEP 9: The finished ends of the necklace with clasp.

# MAKING THE BRACELET

1. Cut 20" of stringing wire.

2. Thread a crimp bead on and center it on the wire length.

3. Match ends of the wire together and pass both through a clamshell bead tip from the inside. Close the clamshell bead tip.

4. Thread on beads in the following sequence: B-A-B-A-B-A-B-A-B-A.

5. Weave the right-angle pattern from steps 1 through 5 of the necklace Weaving the Pattern instructions (Figure 4-73).

6. Repeat step 3 in reverse order.

7. Thread both wires through the bottom of a clamshell tip.

8. Thread a crimp bead on one wire, tie off wires against the crimp bead and trim wires close to the knot.

9. Close clamshell with pliers.

10. Repeat steps 8 and 9 from the Finishing the Necklace instructions to attach the clasp.

# MAKING THE EARRINGS

1. Cut two pieces of wire 10" long. Set one piece aside.

2. Thread beads onto one wire in the following sequence: C-D-C-D-C-D-C-D.

FIGURE 4-75

3. Center the beads on the wire, pass end of wire through the first C bead from the opposite direction and pull up snugly (Figure 4-75).

4. Split wires and thread onto each (Figure 4-75): D-C-D.

5. Bring wire ends together and pass both wires through one 8mm topaz bead and one 4mm bronze round bead (Figure 4-75).

6. Thread both wires through the bottom of a clamshell tip.

7. Thread a crimp bead on one wire, tie off wires against the crimp bead and trim wires close to the knot.

8. Close the clamshell with pliers.

9. Bend the bar of the clamshell through the loop on one earring finding.

10. Repeat steps 2 through 9 for the second earring.

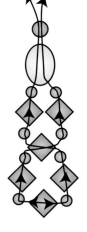

## MATERIALS

- 4 grams dark red 11° seed beads
- 2 grams gold-plated 11° seed beads
- 10mm round gold filigree bead
- 108" brown Silamide thread
- Scissors
- Gem glue
- Bead sorting dish or cloth

## WEAVING STITCHES

# PEYOTE BRACELET

Once you have mastered the basics of peyote stitch given on page 36, it's time to do a piece with a pattern. This is a simple repeat pattern using two colors of beads. Start at the bottom of the piece and pay particular attention to which color of bead to thread on next. Once you have the pattern set, you should be able to tell by looking which bead comes next.

# WEAVING THE BRACELET

1. Single-thread the needle with as much thread as you can handle and tie a stop bead on the end, leaving an 8" tail.

2. Thread on one gold, one red, one gold and five red beads, following the beading pattern (Figure 4-76), beginning in the lower left corner of the pattern. These beads will become the first two rows.

3. Thread on one red bead and pass back through the seventh bead picked up in the first row. Pull snugly.

4. Thread on a second red bead and pass through the fifth bead picked up.

5. Thread on a gold bead and pass through the third bead picked up; it should be a gold one.

6. Thread on a gold bead and pass through the first bead picked up; it should be another gold one. You have completed the third row.

7. Follow the pattern closely, as shown below, and weave a length 1" shorter than you want the bracelet to be. Try to end your weaving in the middle of a pattern, just as you started.

8. Start new threads using one of the techniques given in Chapter 2, page 20. Work in thread tails.

FIGURE 4-76

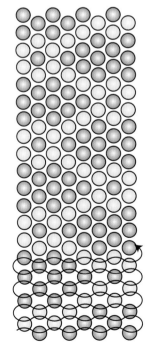

STEP 7: The woven pattern.

# FINISHING THE BRACELET

1. Thread on five red beads, one gold, the 10mm gold filigree bead and one red bead when you get to the end of the weaving.

2. Skip the last red bead and pass back through the 10mm filigree bead and the gold-plated seed bead.

3. Thread on five red beads and pass needle into end row of weaving on the other side of the band.

4. Work needle through the end of band to other side.

5. Pass thread through the beads from steps 1 through 4 again. Repeat a third time if you can.

6. Work thread back into band, tie off with a few half-hitch knots, glue if desired and trim thread ends.

7. Remove the stop bead from other end and place the thread tail in needle.

8. Thread on five red beads, one gold-plated bead and enough red beads to pass easily around the 10mm filigree bead on the other end.

9. Pass back through the gold bead.

10. Thread on five red beads and pass needle into the end row of weaving on the other side of the band.

11. Work needle through end of band to other side.

12. Pass thread through the beads from steps 7 through 10 again. Repeat a third time if you can.

13. Work thread back into band, tie off with a few half-hitch knots, glue if desired and trim thread ends for the finished look shown below.

STEP 13: The finished ends with ball-and-loop clasp.

## MATERIALS

- 2 wooden candlesticks
- 8 grams blue aurora borealis 11° seed beads
- 8 grams blue aurora borealis matte 11° seed beads
- 3 grams bronze metallic 11° seed beads
- 1 spool brown Silamide thread
- Size 10 or 12 beading needle
- Scissors
- Bead sorting dish or cloth

# SQUARE STITCH CANDLEHOLDERS

These wooden candlesticks have an inset place on them that is perfect for a square-stitched band. Because it is difficult to judge how long to make something when you are getting started with a weave, a simple stripe pattern seems the best way to go. That way, you can measure as you weave.

# INSTRUCTIONS

1. Single-thread the needle with as much thread as you can handle and tie a stop bead within 6" of end of thread.

2. Thread on beads in the following sequence: two blue AB seed beads, one bronze, two blue matte seed beads, one bronze, three blue AB, one bronze, two blue matte, one bronze and two blue AB.

3. Push beads up against the stop bead.

4. Refer to the basic square stitch instructions and the pattern here (Figure 4-77) and weave enough rows to fit exactly around the candlestick. The sample has 50 rows. You may work from either direction, but start at the bottom of the pattern.

5. Place the woven band around candlestick, as shown below, and weave the band ends together using the same stitch.

6. Work thread tails through the weaving, just as you would for anything else, and trim the thread end.

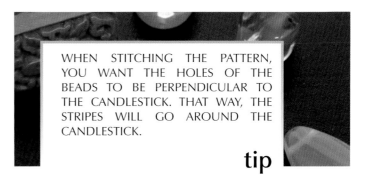

WHEN STITCHING THE PATTERN, YOU WANT THE HOLES OF THE BEADS TO BE PERPENDICULAR TO THE CANDLESTICK. THAT WAY, THE STRIPES WILL GO AROUND THE CANDLESTICK.

**tip**

STEP 5: When the ends are woven together, there is no recognizable seam between the beginning and end.

FIGURE 4-77

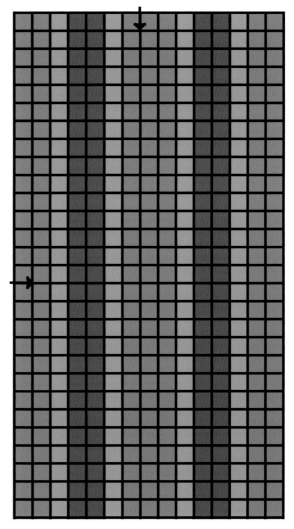

## MATERIALS

- 300 gold 6° seed beads (A)

- 360 silver-lined clear 5mm or 6mm bugle beads (B)

- 2,560 (25 grams) silver-lined clear 11° seed beads (C)

- 20 clear crystal 6mm bicone beads (D)

- 10 yards white Beadalon™ DandyLine™ .006"-diameter thread

- Gem-Tac™ Permanent Adhesive

- Size 10 beading needle

- Scissors

- Bead sorting dish or cloth

## WEAVING STITCHES

# NETTING WINE BOTTLE COVER

Netting works well to cover various articles and to make something like a common wine bottle a little more elegant for that special dinner party. One cover will fit most sizes of bottles because it expands and contracts so well.

# WEAVING THE PATTERN

**1.** Single-thread the needle with as much thread as you can handle.

**2.** Tie one 11° clear seed bead within 6" of the end of the thread in a simple overhand knot.

**3.** Refer to the Bead Key and thread on beads in the following sequence (Figure 4-78): A-C-C-C-B-C-C-C. Repeat eight more times, making nine sections.

**4.** Thread on A-C-C-C-C-C-A-C-C-C-C-C-A-D-A-C, skip the last C bead and pass needle back through the rest of the beads strung in this step (Figure 4-79). Pull thread snug. This is the fringe for the bottom of the piece.

**5.** Thread on C-C-C-B-C-C-C-A-C-C-C-B-C-C-C and then pass thread through the second A bead above the fringe (Figure 4-80).

**6.** Repeat step 5 up the strand (Figure 4-81) until you have four half-diamonds.

**7.** Finish off row with C-C-C-B-C-C-C-A-C, skip the last C bead and pass back through the A bead (Figure 4-81). You are now ready to start the third row.

**8.** Thread on C-C-C-B-C-C-C-A-C-C-C-B-C-C-C, and not counting the first A bead at the top, pass the needle through the second A bead from the previous row (Figure 4-82).

**9.** Repeat step 8 three more times (Figure 4-82).

**10.** Thread on C-C-C-B-C-C-C and the fringe beads (A-C-C-C-C-C-A-C-C-C-C-C-A-D-A-C), skip the last C bead and pass back through the fringe beads, just as in step 4 (Figure 4-79). You are ready to start the next row.

**11.** Continue making rows until you have 20 points at the top (one row is half a point) and 20 fringes on the bottom.

**12.** Fold the piece around the bottle until the edges meet and you come out of the last fringe, thread on C-C-C-B-C-C-C and pass through the A bead on the other edge of woven section (Figure 4-83, next page).

**13.** Thread on C-C-C-B-C-C-C and pass back to the first edge of the piece through the A bead (Figure 4-83). Continue back and forth in this manner, across and up the piece, pulling the thread snugly as you go.

**14.** Come out the last A bead and tie off the threads securely against that bead. If you have a lot of thread left, do not cut it off.

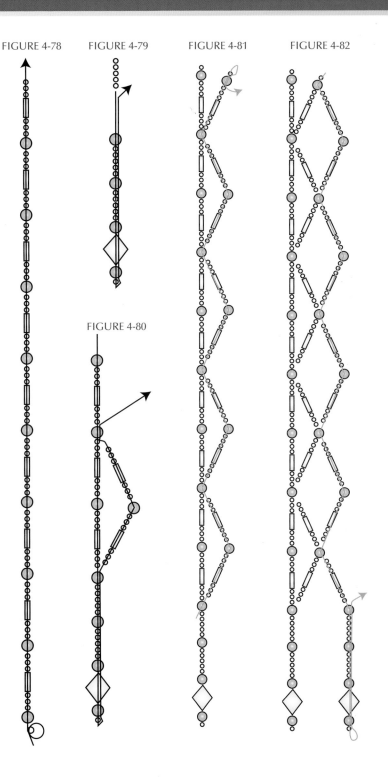

FIGURE 4-78    FIGURE 4-79    FIGURE 4-81    FIGURE 4-82

FIGURE 4-80

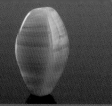

# MAKING THE NECKBAND

1. Bring needle through the top C bead.

2. Thread on C-A-C and pass through the top C bead on the next point. Continue around the piece in this manner (Figure 4-84) until you get back to where you started, pulling the thread snugly as you go.

3. Pass through the first point (C) bead again and then through the first C and A beads strung in step 2 (Figure 4-85).

4. As you exit the A bead, thread on C-C-A-C-C, loop around and pass back through the A bead in the same direction (Figure 4-85).

5. Pass through the remaining C added in step 2 and the next point (C) bead (Figure 4-85).

6. Repeat steps 3 through 5 around the neck of the piece, making loops around each A bead from the previous round (Figure 4-85).

7. Thread on two C beads and pass through the top A bead in the first loop (Figure 4-86). Repeat around the top, pull up thread snugly and tie off securely.

FIGURE 4-83

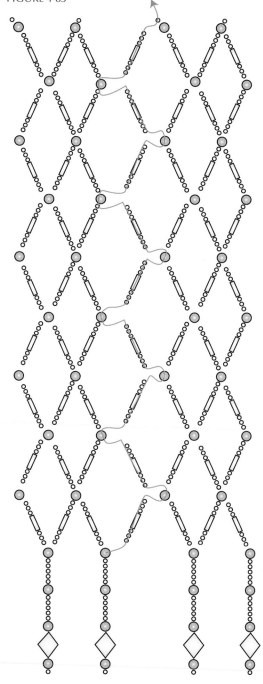

FIGURE 4-84

FIGURE 4-85

FIGURE 4-86

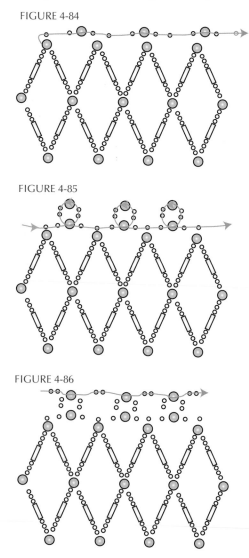

[1]

[2]

[3]

[4]

[1] This necklace by the author combines wedge-shaped alunite beads with large, round sponge coral and Bali silver beads to make a stunning one-strand necklace.

[2] This red-and-turquoise necklace uses a three-strand clasp. Each strand is progressively longer than the previous one so it hangs correctly. It also uses a strand spacer to keep the strands separated.

[3] Amanda Denton of Hipchick Beads chose black-and-white lampworked beads and Swarovski crystals to use in her beaded watch. Because watch faces for beading are easy to find, you can make a watch to match every outfit.

[4] This piece by Dawn Harbor features her handmade beads on a necklace of macramé cords. Multiple strands were knotted together to make this striking piece.

**[5]** In this piece, Stella Maris used gray pearls with common hardware washers to make an attractive double-strand necklace. Stella is a wire worker and this piece uses one of her handmade clasps.

**[6]** Zipper pulls are useful accessories on clothing, purses, suitcases or anything else that uses a zipper or has a place to attach a clasp. For these zipper pulls, a few large beads were strung with smaller beads on heavy thread or lightweight stringing wire. The strands were tied off in a clamshell bead tip, which was then attached to a lobster claw clasp.

**[7]** You can purchase decorative bookmarks like this at craft and bead shops or make some of your own from heavy wire. Attach a strand of your favorite beads strung on stringing wire and wow them at the bookstore.

**[8]** This necklace by Stella Maris used a New York City subway token and a coin—both with holes—for a toggle clasp and as part of the pendant. Note the beaded loop used for the other half of the clasp.

[5]

[6]

[7]
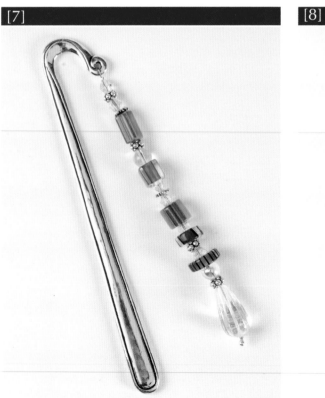

[8]

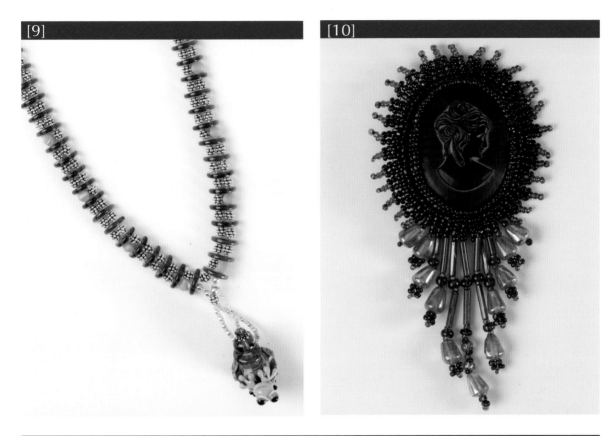

[9]

[10]

[11]

**[9]** This two-hole bead necklace, which first appeared in *Jewelry Crafts Magazine* and is made by the author, features a lampworked frog and vessel bead by Bindy Lambell. The double strand gives the necklace weight so doesn't look too skimpy to hold the vessel.

**[10]** Michele Emerson-Roberts chose a cameo for her cabochon brooch. She did many rows of decorative beading around the cabochon and a spiky outer row. The piece is further enhanced by the use of fringe at the bottom.

**[11]** The centerpiece of this project is a magnificent glass horse head bead made by lampworker Kathy Johnson. The detail she gets in her beads is astounding. No photograph can do them justice.

# RESOURCES

## BEADS
**Fire Mountain Gems and Beads**
1 Fire Mountain Way
Grants Pass, OR 97526-2373
(800) 423-2319
www.firemountaingems.com

**Glass Garden**
413 Division St.
Northfield, MN 55057
(507) 645-0301
www.glassgardenbeads.com

**Jay's Indian Arts, Inc.**
2227 E. 7th Ave.
Flagstaff, AZ 86004
(800) 736-6314
www.JaysIndianArts.com

**Morning Light Emporium**
P.O. Box 92
Paonia, CO 81428
(800) 392-0365
www.mlebeads.com

**Rings & Things**
P.O. Box 450
214 N. Wall St., Suite 990
Spokane, WA 99210-0450
(509) 624-8565
www.rings-things.com

**Rio Grande**
7500 Bluewater Road NW
Albuquerque, NM 87121-1962
(800) 545-6566
www.riogrande.com

**Wild Things**
21771 Sky High Blvd.
Pine Grove, CA 95665
(209) 296-8447
www.wildthingsbeads.com

## GLUES
**Beacon Adhesives**
124 Mac Questen Parkway South
Mount Vernon, NY 10550
(914) 699-3400
www.beacon1.com

## FINDINGS AND STRINGING WIRES
**Beadalon**
Wire and Cable Specialties
205 Carter Drive
West Chester, PA 19382
(866) 423-2325
www.beadalon.com

**Westrim Crafts**
7855 Hayvenhurst Ave.
Van Nyes, CA 91406
(800) 727-2727
www.westrimcrafts.com

## GEMSTONE CABOCHONS
**One-of-a-Kind Rock Shop**
Highway 76 Strip #2855
Branson, MO 65616
(877) 331-0011
www.1ofaknd.com

# CONTRIBUTORS

**Donnie Cripe** (Potawatomi instructions) works and shares her beading knowledge at Hardies Beads in Quartzsite, Arizona. She loves to bead in her spare time.

**Amanda Denton** (Black-and-White Beaded Watch) has been a beader for nearly 11 years. Her designs are usually bright and chunky. Amy and her husband, Tony, own Bead Creative, 906-1/2 42nd St., Des Moines, Iowa 50312, and run an Internet store at hipchickbeads.com.

**Cheryl Erickson** (Lacy Spiral instructions) is a professional bead artist and national beading instructor whose work has been featured in books, galleries and national tours. Cheryl, who has been beading since 1971, founded the Iowa Bead Society, hosts a Web site (www.artisticbead.com) and owns a bead store:

> Artistic Bead, Inc.
> 228 5th St.
> West Des Moines, IA 50265

**Denise Gaffey** (Art Glass Daisy Chain Necklace) is a glass bead artist, and along with silversmith Maurice Sanders, she owns Dema Designs, which specializes in selling both of their artwork. Contact her at:

> P.O. Box 577467
> Modesto, CA 95357-7467
> (209) 985-5033
> www.demadesigns.com

**Dawn Harbor** (Macramé and Glass Bead Necklace) is a glass bead artist and owner of her own beading store at:

> Dawn's Hide and Bead Away
> 521 E. Washington St.
> Iowa City, IA 52240
> Phone: (319) 338-1566
> Web site: www.dawnsbeads.com

**Kathy Johnson** (Horse Head Hat Band) is a glass bead artist and owner of KJ Originals from Burien, Washington. Her marvelous collectable horse beads are signed and dated. Check out her Web site (www.equisglass.com) or e-mail her at glass-expressions@worldnet.att.net or kjoriginals@seanet.com.

**Bindy Lambell** (Frog Vessel Necklace and Spiral Rope Jewelry Set) is a glass bead artist (a.k.a. The Mad Beader) from California. Find her Web site at www.bindy.com or e-mail her at bindylambell@yahoo.com.

**Stella Maris** (Subway Token Necklace and Pearls and Washers Necklace) is a bead and wire artist who lives in Fort Lauderdale, Florida, where she works on a yacht. She likes to include unusual things in her beadwork. She is author Carole Rodgers' niece.

**Denise Miller** (Copper Sparkles Necklace) is a polymer clay bead artist and instructor from Omaha, Nebraska. She exhibits and sells her work at bead shows throughout the Midwest. Contact her via e-mail at denise@dmillerdesignstudio.com.

**Sharon Peters** (Lobster Bead Necklace and Cat Collar) is a glass bead artist who has been specializing in the bright and the wacky since birth. Her whimsical beads will make you chuckle. You can view them at www.smartassglass.com. E-mail her at sharon.peters@smartassglass.com or call her at (510) 865-2138.

**Michele Emerson-Roberts** (Beaded Cameo Brooch) is a multifaceted designer with a love of paper/book arts, beading, polymer clay and painting. She is an award-winning oil, acrylic and watercolor artist. Michele lives in Arizona. Find out more about her at www.micheleemersonroberts.com.